AUTHOR	CLASS No.
	822.91
TITLE	
....	BOOK No.
....	46435192

MYSTERY AT ABBOTS MEAD

A PLAY IN THREE ACTS

BY

WILFRED MASSEY

Licensed by the Lord Chamberlain for public performance. An acting fee is payable in advance in respect of each and every performance of this play, (See next page). No presentation of any kind may lawfully be given unless the copyright-owner's permission has previously been obtained.

If an unauthorised performance has inadvertently taken place; the matter should be regularised at once by sending details to the address below as soon as possible.

Purchase orders for scripts
Applications to perform
Payments of fees and
All other correspondence relating to this play should be
addressed to THE PUBLISHER :

WILFRED MASSEY

"Southwood" 38, Tilsworth Road,

Beaconsfield. (Bucks.)

COPYRIGHT

THIS PUBLICATION IS THE COPYRIGHT OF WILFRED MASSEY

Performance Fees

The fee for the presentation of this play by amateur companies is on sliding-scale, based on estimated gross receipts, and varying from £1.1.0 to a maximum of £4.4.0 each performance. The copyright-owners will try to meet the reasonable needs of the Drama Group concerned with regard to the amount of fee payable in their case, and will supply an Application Form on request.

The royalties payable by professional companies are by arrangement with WILFRED MASSEY PUBLICATIONS (address previous page).

Permission to Perform

All parties concerned in the presentation of a play protected by the Copyright Act of 1956, whether actors, their fellow-members of a Society, proprietors or lessors of a theatre or hall, etc. should satisfy themselves that permission to perform has been given, as any or all of them may be liable in case of infringement. Unauthorised presentation can include —

"PRIVATE PERFORMANCES"

"PLAY - READINGS"

"DRESS REHEARSALS"

(All so-called) given before an audience, no matter how small, and the following factors do not excuse infringement—

That no charge is made for admission.

That the audience consists only of fellow-members of a particular Group or invited guests.

That the proceeds are for charity or the Society's own funds, these being the purposes for which almost all non-professional performances are given.

CHARACTERS

(in the order of their appearance)

HOWARD CARSON

ELSA MILBURN

GRAHAM PETERS

MILLIE

MARGARET PRESTWOOD

THELMA TRANSOM

LAURA HARRINGTON

ANNETTE FIELDING

DETECTIVE-INSPECTOR KERSHAW

C.I.D., New Scotland Yard.

The Scene throughout is a room at Abbot's Mead

Convalescent Home.

Act I.

AN EARLY EVENING IN AUTUMN

Act II.

Scene 1. THE FOLLOWING MORNING

Scene 2. LATER THE SAME MORNING

Act III.

Scene 1. THE SAME NIGHT

Scene 2. THE FOLLOWING MORNING

SETTING

The french window UPSTAGE R. need not be practical as it stands opened outward throughout the play. The window in the back wall R. should consist of enough casements to take up most of the width of the wall. If, alternatively, crossed tapes are used to give a leaded light effect, these should not be so close together as to make the 'panes' too small. The window should be high enough to reveal the heads of people seen beyond. The backing beyond is sky with, if desired, some flowers, or flowering shrubs or trees, but it should be simple and not 'heavy'. Upstage L. is an open entrance with an arched or square top; beyond is passage backing. There is a door Down R., opening inwards, with passage backing beyond. A few pictures or prints are on the walls and, in particular, there is one on the R. wall downstage (See Production Notes about this). A fireplace could be in the LEFT wall, if desired, but it is not required by the action.

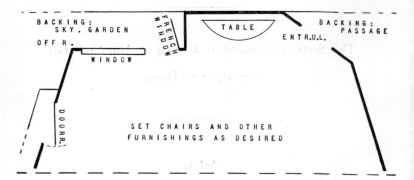

BASIC GROUND PLAN

FURNITURE

The room is furnished comfortably, in either traditional or contemporary style. There should be light, modern armchairs and not heavy easy-chairs, and if a settee would restrict the acting area too much, there is no need to have one. One or two small tables, including a low coffee-table. Wall lighting fixtures, table lamps or standard, as desired.

ACT ONE

SCENE : The lounge at Abbot's Mead, a convalescent home in the country. An early evening in the autumn.

(As the CURTAIN *rises* HOWARD CARSON *is seen seated, working morosely at weaving a small basket which is on the table in front of him. Although a young man his mood is anything but one of high spirits, no doubt because he is having a lot of difficulty in interlacing one of the lengths; he has several tries at threading it through, then loses his temper and gives it a violent jab. He curses it visibly under his breath, then exerts a great effort of self-control and starts to do it very carefully and painstakingly. He registers relief and satisfaction and has almost succeeded when . .)*

ELSA (OFF L.): Howard (HOWARD *starts violently at the shock and sends the basket flying. He sits back, too shattered even to curse)* Howard! Where are you?

HOWARD : In here. Where else would I be ? *(He runs his fingers through his hair, looking haggard, then gets out a cigarette pack. He opens it. It is empty. This is the last straw. He slumps back in his chair and tosses the packet away in dull, resigned despair.* ELSA MILBURN *enters U.L. She is a pretty girl, attractively dressed in casual style for indoors)*

ELSA : Oh, there you are. Miss Prestwood thought you might have gone for a walk.

HOWARD : Miss Prestwood, for once in her life, was wrong then, wasn't she?

ELSA : And Graham said you'd been thinking about it, too.

HOWARD : I did. And when I'd thought about it, d'you know what I came up with? That going for a walk would bore me rigid and that sitting in here would bore me rigid. So I decided to be bored rigid right here without giving myself any trouble.

ELSA *(laughs):* Poor old Howard. Got one of your moods again, have you? *(She picks up the basket)* What's this? I know—your occupational therapy.

HOWARD : I've got another name for it.

ELSA : Miss Prestwood said it would do you a lot of good.

HOWARD : Miss Prestwood is a - - -

ELSA : Howard !

HOWARD : It's all very well for you! You haven't been put on to basket-making.

ELSA : I haven't had a nervous breakdown. You have. *(She puts the basket on the table)*

HOWARD : And if I see much more of that confounded basket I'll have another! All last week I was on the gardening lark. Before you know it she'll have me working a hand-loom and making pottery! (GRAHAM PETERS enters U.L. *He too is young but he walks a little heavily and with the aid of a shooting-stick. He is the jovial type, whose favourite mode of address is 'old boy'. He smokes a pipe and watches with amusement*)

ELSA : It might do you good. It might make you relax and improve your temper.

HOWARD : I didn't come here to have my temper improved! (*Disgustedly, as he jabs the loose strand impatiently—*) Convalescent Homes!

ELSA : Miss Prestwood's doing a very good job as matron, considering all the difficulties she's had. And it's a very good Convalescent Home.

GRAHAM (*heartily*): The best. (*Giving ELSA a hug*) It brought us together.

HOWARD : When you two have finished gazing at each other with that gruesome love-light shining in your eyes, perhaps you'll tell me what you're hanging about here for.

GRAHAM : Well, actually, old boy, I came to ask Elsa whether she'd like a walk to the station.

ELSA : But can you manage it, Graham?

GRAHAM : Oh, I think so. The old leg's practically as good as new again.

ELSA : Actually I was going to ask Howard whether he'd like to walk down to the station.

HOWARD : What does everybody want to go walking to stations for?

ELSA : Howard! You know who's coming.

HOWARD : Who? Oh, *her*.

ELSA : The exercise will do you good.

HOWARD : Exercise never does me good.

ELSA : Oh, don't be such a grouch, Howard.

HOWARD : Look, why don't the three of you go and give your romance the chance to blossom?

ELSA : The three of us?

HOWARD : You, him and the shooting-stick.

ELSA : When you're like this it's just a waste of time talking to you. (*Going L.*)

HOWARD : Are you going to make her walk all the way here?

ELSA : Of course not. The shooting-brake's parked at the station. I'll get my coat, Graham. (*She exits U.L. GRAHAM sits, carefully stretching out his injured leg. The telephone-bell rings*)

GRAHAM : What d'you think she'll be like, old boy?

HOWARD : I wouldn't know.

GRAHAM : I can just picture her, a vision of beauty in her trim nurse's uniform, always ready with soothing words as she lays her gentle hand on your fevered brow.

HOWARD : If she's anything like the nurses *I've* ever had she'll be a hatchet-faced old dragon with a mania for keeping your windows and your bowels open.

GRAHAM (*laughs*): Well, I'd better get my thick stick if we're going to climb that hill to the station. (*As he goes L., MILLIE enters U.L. She carries a handbag and her coat is slung over her shoulder but she still wears her apron*) Telephone, Millie.

MILLIE : I know, I heard it. (*GRAHAM exits U.L.*) Just my luck— half a minute later and I'd 'a been gone. What with that cat of Maggie Prestwood's smellin' the place out, an' that loony Miss Transom going on—'Fetch me this, fetch me that—do me corsets up'—Oh, I've just about had enough tonight, I can tell you. (*Into 'phone, without any pause for breath—*) Hallo, Abbot's Mead Convalescent Home . . . Yes. Do you want to speak to Miss Prestwood? . . . Who, then? Oh, her. No, not yet. We're expectin' her any time. Who's speakin'? . . . Hallo. (*Listens, then shrugs. GRAHAM enters U.L. with a stout walking-stick. MILLIE puts on her coat*) Well, I'm off.

GRAHAM : Where are you going?

MILLIE : It's my evenin' off and my friend'll be waitin' at the 'bus stop. We're goin' to the flicks.

GRAHAM : Not tonight, surely?

MILLIE (*defiantly*): Yes — tonight. An' if Maggie Prestwood doesn't like it she can flippin' well lump it! (*Making for DOOR R.*)

MISS PRESTWOOD (*OFF L.*): Millie.

MILLIE (*in disgust*): Isn't it marvellous!

GRAHAM (*chuckling*): Too late, Millie. No flicks for you tonight.

HOWARD : Why not? If it's her night off it's her night off.

GRAHAM : Not tonight, it isn't. Miss Prestwood was telling Elsa that Millie's relief hasn't turned up. (*MISS PRESTWOOD enters U.L. She is a woman of neat appearance, wearing a dark dress, perhaps of navy-blue, with white collar and cuffs. Her manner is kindly and only just stops short of being prim*)

MISS PRESTWOOD : Oh, there you are, Millie. I want . . . What are you doing with your coat on?

MILLIE : It's my night off!

MISS PRESTWOOD : But I've explained about that, Millie. I simply can't spare you tonight—not with her coming.

MILLIE (*obstinately*): I'm very sorry, Miss Prestwood.

MISS PRESTWOOD : Now Millie — do be reasonable.

MILLIE : I'm not paid to be reasonable.

MISS PRESTWOOD : But I *told* you. I expected that new daily to come and help out but she hasn't turned up.

MILLIE : Can't help that. It's my night off.

MISS PRESTWOOD (*with prim firmness*): Well, I'm very sorry, Millie, but you can't have it.

MILLIE (*almost unable to believe her ears*): What was that you said, Miss Prestwood?

MISS PRESTWOOD : I said you can't have this evening off. (*MILLIE is too affronted to speak for some moments. Then she extends her hand*)

MILLIE : Cards, please.

MISS PRESTWOOD : Cards?

MILLIE : I want me cards.

MISS PRESTWOOD : You can't mean that, Millie.

MILLIE : Can't I? (*With some haughtiness*—) Well, I happen to be funny that way, Miss Prestwood, 'cos when I say I want me cards I mean I want me cards. (ELSA *enters U.L., wearing her coat*)

GRAHAM : Now look, Millie—be a good girl. Help Miss Prestwood out tonight and I'm sure she'll make it up to you later. (*Giving* MILLIE *a hug*)

MILLIE (*wavering*): Well —

GRAHAM : That's my girl.

MILLIE : Okay, then.

MISS PRESTWOOD (*beaming*): Oh, thank you, Millie. Now, if you'll come along with me we'll finish getting Miss Lorrimer's old bedroom ready.

MILLIE (*going L.*): But mind — this doesn't mean I can be made a convenience of. Any more messin' about with my night off an' I'm havin' me cards. (*She exits U.L., followed by* MISS PRESTWOOD)

ELSA : We'd better be getting along, Graham, if we're going to meet that train. We don't want to keep her waiting. (*She exits by french window*)

GRAHAM : Righty-o. (*To* HOWARD, *who is moodily working at his basket*—) Well, keep up the good work, old boy, and if you make a really good job of your little basket perhaps Miss Prestwood will upgrade you to making a bumper-size picnic hamper. Ha-ha! (*He laughs heartily then ducks as* HOWARD *starts to hurl the basket at his head. Still laughing he exits by french window and* OFF R. HOWARD *shuts his eyes and tries to master his feelings. He has cooled off somewhat when* MISS THELMA TRANSOM's *head and shoulders appear at* ENTR. U.L.)

MISS TRANSOM : Psst! (HOWARD *starts with shock and sends his basket flying.* MISS TRANSOM *enters U.L. Middle-aged and weirdly-dressed she alternates between innocent simplicity and witch-like glee. An old-style feather boa is slung round her neck and she wears a scarlet cardigan with a purple dress, or something equally sensational. She carries an open-topped work-bag over one arm*). Where is she?

HOWARD : Who?

MISS TRANSOM : Eh?

HOWARD (*loudly*): I said who?

MISS TRANSOM (*cupping her ear with her hand*): I can't hear you.

HOWARD (*normal tone, getting up*): Oh, never mind, you deaf old . . . basket, where is it? (*Searching around he does not see* MISS TRANSOM *take a hearing-aid from her bag and plug it in the ear which is towards the audience. He picks up his basket, then bellows*—) Why don't you put your hearing-aid in?

MISS TRANSOM (*wincing at the noise*): Don't shout, Mr Carson. I've put my hearing-aid in.

HOWARD (*growling*): Not before time.

MISS TRANSOM : Has she come yet?

HOWARD : 'Mm? No, not yet. Any time now.

MISS TRANSOM : Well, she can't come too soon for me. Do you know the latest? Treacle with porage!

HOWARD : Eh?

MISS TRANSOM : That's how they eat porage in Yorkshire. With *treacle* on it. Or so Miss Prestwood says. Do you know what I told her? "You try putting your treacle on their porage North of the Border, Miss Prestwood", I said, "and you'll soon see what they'll do with it". She was going to the pictures tonight, you know.

HOWARD : Miss Prestwood?

MISS TRANSOM : No. no, no. I'm talking about Millie. But she couldn't because of you-know-who coming. (*In a very conspiratorial manner—*) Would you like me to tell you a secret?

HOWARD : No, but that won't stop you.

MISS TRANSOM : I saw them kissing in the rose-arbour.

HOWARD : Miss Prestwood and Millie?

MISS TRANSOM : No, no, no. Mr. Peters and Elsa Milburn. Really Mr Carson, you're not very quick in the uptake are you? Do you think they're in love?

HOWARD : I wouldn't know. (*Reaching for his basket*) And now, if you don't mind, Miss Transom, I've got a lot of work I don't want to do.

MISS TRANSOM : Then I won't stop you, because I know what it's like, making baskets. Very tricky at first, until you get the hang of it. You feel all fingers and thumbs, don't you? They had me making baskets for ages, but that was in dear Miss Lorrimer's time and I've got past all that now. But you will let me know when she comes, won't you, because I've got a lot of things I want to speak to her about. Treacle in porage—the very idea! (*She exits U.L. HOWARD gazes at the basket in disgust for some moments then wearily tosses it aside. He heaves a deep sigh and sits back, sprawling. Presently his eyes fall on the cigarette-box on the table near him and he exerts himself enough to open it and take out a cigarette. He puts it between his lips in a very lackadaisical way. LAURA HARRINGTON enters from OFF R. and comes to french window. She is an attractive girl, nicely dressed for outdoors and she carries a week-end case. HOWARD slaps each pocket in search for matches then, finding none, wearily looks round for some. As he turns his head he catches sight of LAURA. He glances at her briefly, then ignores her and goes on looking for matches*)

LAURA : Is this Abbot's Mead?

HOWARD : Didn't you see that dirty great signboard at the main gateway?

LAURA : I didn't come as far as the gateway. I came in by a little door further down the road.

HOWARD (*still not looking at her*): Then you shouldn't have done.

LAURA : Why not?

HOWARD : Because that's the tradesmen's entrance and you're too
late to be delivering the fish . . . Why does nobody think of
having any matches around the place?

LAURA : I think I'm expected.

HOWARD : No you're not. The only party who's expected here
tonight is an old dragon of a . . . Good lor' ! (*He gets up
quickly*) You're not *her*?

LAURA : I'm Laura Harrington.

HOWARD : Then you *are* her!

LAURA : So I take it you are expecting me.

HOWARD : We certainly are. You might say we've all been on
tenter hooks waiting for you to arrive. (*His manner indicates
that her arrival gives him no pleasure*)

LAURA (*with a slightly puzzled smile*): Well, that's very flattering
but I can't think why they should.

HOWARD (*still far from graciously*): Well, come in. (*He takes her
case and sets it aside while* LAURA *comes downstage*) You're a
bit early, aren't you? Someone's gone to meet your train.

LAURA : Somebody gave me a lift from the station.

HOWARD : I wonder if Peters and Elsa have gone through the gate
yet. I suppose I ought to 'phone through to the porter. Yes, I
will. (*He picks up the telephone*) Hallo . . . Hallo. (*He turns and
catches sight of* LAURA *putting her hand over her eyes*) Are you
all right? (LAURA *sways.* HOWARD *quickly replaces the 'phone and
crosses to her.* LAURA *lurches forward*) Hey — steady! (*He is just
in time to catch her as she collapses. He puts her in the nearest
armchair, drops on one knee and puts her head back.* MILLIE
enters U.L. without her coat)

MILLIE (*calling back*): It's my night off, Miss Transom, and I'm
only obligin'—that doesn't mean runnin' round after you!

HOWARD : Millie!

MILLIE : Why, Mr Carson — that isn't—

HOWARD : Yes, it's Miss Harrington. She seems to have fainted.
Get some water and tell Miss Prestwood.

MILLIE : Yes — yes, okay. (*She hurries out U.L.* ELSA *has appeared
at french window and* GRAHAM *follows*)

ELSA : Laura! (*She comes quickly downstage to* LAURA)

GRAHAM : What happened?

HOWARD : She just came in, we were talking, then she fainted.
(*He gets to his feet leaving* ELSA *to tend* LAURA) It would have
to be me she picked on!

GRAHAM : Did she say anything about not feeling well?

HOWARD : No, not a word. What brought you two back?

GRAHAM : Elsa thought she saw somebody come in by the tradesmen's door.

HOWARD : That's right. How is she, Elsa?

ELSA : Just the same. (*As the three look down at* LAURA *a girl
appears from* OFF R. *She wears a bright red coat or white mac
or something equally noticeable. Her hands are in her pockets
and she stands looking at* LAURA, *her face expressionless. Pre-*

sently LAURA's *head moves to one side)* I think she's coming round.

GRAHAM : We'd better send for Miss Prestwood.

HOWARD : It's all right — Millie's gone.

MISS PRESTWOOD (OFF L.): Come along, Millie.

GRAHAM : Here she is.

ELSA : Laura, Laura — wake up. (MISS PRESTWOOD *enters* U.L., *followed by* MILLIE, *who carries a basin and a glass of water)*

MISS PRESTWOOD : How is she?

ELSA : She moved her head. I thought she was coming round but she hasn't (MISS PRESTWOOD *takes a face-cloth from the basin, wrings it out and presses it to* LAURA's *temples.* GRAHAM *and* HOWARD *have moved away and both* ELSA *and* MISS PRESTWOOD *are at* LAURA's *chair, so that the girl at the window is not masked. She watches, still impassively. Presently* LAURA's *head moves, first to one side then the other)*

ELSA : Her colour's coming back.

MISS PRESTWOOD : Yes, she's reviving. *(The girl, with a last look at* LAURA, *moves away, not too quickly and not furtively and exits* OFF R. *Nobody has seen her.* LAURA's *eyelids flicker and she finally opens her eyes)*

ELSA : Laura . . . Laura, do you feel better?

LAURA : My head's swimming a bit. What happened?

MISS PRESTWOOD : You fainted, Miss Harrington. Nothing to worry about.

LAURA : Are you Miss Prestwood?

MISS PRESTWOOD : Yes, I am. Now, have a drink of water. *(Takes glass from* MILLIE *and puts it to* LAURA's *lips)* There — is that better!

LAURA : Yes. Sorry to be such a nuisance. (MILLIE *takes the glass from* MISS PRESTWOOD)

MISS PRESTWOOD *(soothingly)*: Don't worry about it, dear.

ELSA : You'll soon be all right, Laura.

LAURA *(looks at* ELSA, *clearly puzzled)*: I'm afraid I don't . . .

ELSA : Laura, dear — you know who this is.

LAURA : I'm sorry I—

ELSA : Elsa.

LAURA : Elsa? *(It is obvious that the name means nothing to her.* ELSA *looks in some concern at* MISS PRESTWOOD, *then at* GRAHAM) I seem to know your face—but— *(Tries to remember, then shakes her head)* No I'm sorry.

HOWARD *(to* GRAHAM): I thought they were at school together.

GRAHAM : Yes, they were.

LAURA : School? . . . Elsa Milburn!

ELSA : That's right, darling.

LAURA : Of course. *(She smiles her apology)* Stupid of me not to recognize you right away, but it's been quite a few years since we saw each other.

ELSA : Since we saw each other, yes, But . . *(She hesitates.* LAURA *notices the puzzled look on her face, then sees* HOWARD *and*

GRAHAM *also exchanging puzzled looks. Then she sees* MISS PRESTWOOD *looking at her in some concern)*

LAURA : What's the matter?

MISS PRESTWOOD (*soothingly*): Nothing. That long journey from Dublin has tired you. You'll be all right after a good night's rest.

LAURA : There's nothing wrong with me really. Apart from those faints.

MISS PRESTWOOD : Those? You mean you fainted before this?

LAURA : Yest. It was on the boat coming over from Waterford. I remember feeling faint and I tried to get up on deck for some fresh air but I never got there. I must have been out quite a while because when I came round we'd got in at Fishguard.

MISS PRESTWOOD : Did you feel any after-effects?

LAURA : Well, my head hurt. One or two of the people who took me to the First Aid room ashore said they'd seen me bang it pretty hard against a rail when I fell . . . Just there. (MISS PRESTWOOD *gently fingers the spot)*

MISS PRESTWOOD : Does it hurt much?

LAURA : Yes, quite a bit.

MISS PRESTWOOD : I think you'd better lie down as soon as possible, dear. Millie, go and get Miss Harrington's bed ready.

MILLIE : Yes, okay. (*Taking the basin and the glass she exits* U.L.)

ELSA : Don't you think you'd better let Doctor Roberts see her?

LAURA : Oh, I'll be all right after a night's rest.

MISS PRESTWOOD : We'll see how you are in the morning. You've brought your things?

LAURA : Just a week-end case. I sent a trunk on by rail. (*She gives a puzzled laugh*) I can't understand why I should faint on the boat like that. I'm not the fainting kind.

MISS PRESTWOOD : Well, I've heard of the motion of a boat causing some people to faint instead of making them seasick. But of course you will know more about that than I do. (LAURA *looks at her sharply)*

LAURA (*guardedly*): Why should I?

MISS PRESTWOOD : Because of your profession.

LAURA : My profession? (*She is not puzzled so much as wary*) I don't know what you mean. (ELSA *and* MISS PRESTWOOD *exchange looks of consternation.* HOWARD *looks puzzled, so does* GRAHAM)

ELSA (*worried*): Miss Prestwood, I think you ought to call Dr. Roberts tonight.

GRAHAM : Yes, so do I.

LAURA : No, no. There's no need to do that.

GRAHAM : Well, I don't know. After all . . . (*He stops)*

LAURA : Well, go on. (*There is a silence*) Look—what's all this about?

HOWARD : He means that concussion can be a tricky thing.

LAURA : Concussion!

MISS PRESTWOOD : Well, perhaps not as bad as that.

LAURA : I tell you I'm all right.

ELSA : But you did faint twice today, darling.

LAURA : Yes. (*She stops, uncertainly*) Only . . .

ELSA : Only what? (MILLIE *enters* U.L.)

LAURA : The second time wasn't like the first. On the boat this morning I — sort of went out fairly suddenly, without feeling faint. But tonight the faintness came gradually. As if . . .

ELSA : Yes?

LAURA (*very thoughtfully*): I don't know.

MILLIE : Miss Harrington's bed's all ready.

MISS PRESTWOOD : Very well, Millie.

MILLIE : An' I forgot to tell you before but there was somebody on the telephone for Miss Harrington.

LAURA (*surprised*): For me?

MISS PRESTWOOD : What did he want?

MILLIE : He just asked if he could speak to Miss Harrington and when I told him she hadn't arrived he rang off.

LAURA : But nobody knows I'm here.

MISS PRESTWOOD : Well, Mr Wetherburn does, of course, but —

LAURA (*overlapping*): Who's Mr Wetherburn?

ELSA : But surely he hasn't come up from London, has he?

MISS PRESTWOOD : Not that I know of. I know — it must have been that man from the County Health Department.

HOWARD : At this hour?

MISS PRESTWOOD : I expect he couldn't get me earlier from the office so he telephoned from his home.

LAURA (*mystified*): What *is* all this?

MISS PRESTWOOD : Nothing to worry about tonight, dear. Now I'm going to get you some warm milk and you can drink it in bed. (*Going L.*) Come with me, Millie. (*She exits* U.L. MILLIE, *looking back, puzzled, at* LAURA, *follows her out*)

LAURA : Who's Mr Wetherburn and what was that about the Health Department? (*She catches the worried look that passes between* GRAHAM *and* ELSA) Look, my head's aching a bit and I know I'm not at my brightest, but there's no need to treat me as though I were a half-wit. Will you please tell me what this is all about?

GRAHAM : Look, Miss Harrington, you seem to have had a pretty rough time. Why not call it a day, get a good night's sleep and in the morning you'll be as good as new again.

LAURA : Who are you?

ELSA : This is Graham, darling — Graham Peters. He's convalescing as well.

LAURA : As well?

ELSA : Like me, I mean. You know about my car crash and having to have a plastic job done on me.

LAURA : I don't know anything about it.

ELSA : But Laura— (*She stops and is silent a moment, then gives a tiny shrug of helplessness*) Anyway, after they'd put me together again I came here for a good long rest. I've been here nearly six weeks.

GRAHAM (*grinning at* LAURA): Yes, it's an ill wind and all that, isn't it? (*She gives him a puzzled look*) Well, what I mean is—if Elsa hadn't had that car crash and I hadn't carved up the old leg— well, I mean we'd neither of us have come to Abbot's Mead and we'd never have met. And that would have been just too bad, wouldn't it, old girl? (*Gives* ELSA *an affectionate hug*)

ELSA (*to* LAURA): One day I'll get him trained out of calling me 'old girl', as if I were his favourite mare or something. This is the character I told you about.

LAURA : You what?

ELSA : In my letter. I told you he was a constructional engineer and he was here because he'd fallen off a staging and broken his leg pretty badly. Don't you remember?

LAURA (*bewildered*): I've never had a letter from you in my life.

ELSA (*equally bewildered*): Laura, you must remember—

LAURA (*overlapping*): I've never seen you or heard anything about you since we left school.

ELSA : We've never met since then, no. But you must have got my letter because you wrote back. You asked me whether Graham and I were engaged.

LAURA : Look — I just haven't any idea what you're talking about. (MISS PRESTWOOD *enters* U.L.)

ELSA (*with a worried look at* GRAHAM): Well, we won't talk about it any more tonight. Perhaps in the—

LAURA (*overlapping, heatedly*): And will you please stop talking to me as though I were a mentally backward child!

MISS PRESTWOOD : Your bed's quite ready, Miss Harrington.

LAURA : I'm not going to bed!

MISS PRESTWOOD : I really think you'd better —

LAURA : Not until I know what this is all about.

MISS PRESTWOOD : We can talk about it in the morning.

LAURA : I want to talk about it now!

HOWARD : Personally, I don't blame her.

LAURA (*turning on him*): And I suppose I ought to know all about you, too!

HOWARD : Oh no. I shouldn't think Elsa would have bothered to mention me in her letter. I'm Howard Carson. I didn't break any arms or legs or anything. I just had nice, tidy nervous break-down.

LAURA : I can guess just how you felt! (*Her anger spends itself. She looks very weary*) Oh, I'm sorry. But I'm so tired. (MISS TRANSOM *enters* U.L.)

MISS TRANSOM : Ah, there you are, Miss Harrington. Millie told me you were here. I can't tell you how much we've been looking forward to your arrival. At last I'll get something done for my stomach. Oh — not that Miss Prestwood isn't very helpful — she is. Very helpful indeed. But it's not the same as having some-body qualified, is it?

LAURA : Qualified? (*This time she is not so much angry as wary*)

MISS TRANSOM (*to* MISS PRESTWOOD): You know, dear, I didn't tell you at the time, because I'm not one to be always complaining, as you know, but the last lot of stomach tablets you gave me didn't suit me at all. I was quite light-headed after I'd taken them.

HOWARD : And before.

MISS PRESTWOOD (to LAURA): This is Miss Transom, our oldest guest.

MISS TRANSOM : Yes, indeed. I was here in Miss Lorrimer's time. She was very strict with us — very strict indeed. More like a schoolmistress than a matron — rules, rules all the time. It drove many of her patients away, and I told her so. But for myself I didn't mind that because after all, she was qualified — like you, Miss Harrington and that makes up for everything—

LAURA (overlapping, tensely): Will you tell me what you mean by me being qualified?

MISS TRANSOM (mildly surprised): There's no need to snap my head off, Miss Harrington.

MISS PRESTWOOD: Miss Harrington has had a long journey and she's very tired. Now I must ask you to go up to your room, Miss Transom. Miss Milburn, will you take her?

ELSA : Yes, of course. (Taking MISS TRANSOM's arm) Come along, Miss Transom.

MISS TRANSOM (stiffly): Oh, very well, if that's your attitude. But if you're not very careful, Miss Prestwood, you'll find yourself getting like Miss Lorrimer and then you'll lose all your guests and go bankrupt, like she did before she had that stroke. (In ENTR. U.L.) And all for the sake of a few stomach-tablets. (ELSA takes her arm and almost pulls her out U.L. LAURA has been lying back in her chair, her eyes shut. The girl in the red coat appears at the french window and stands looking at LAURA, her hands in her pockets. Nobody sees her)

MISS PRESTWOOD : How do you feel now?

LAURA : Not so good. I think perhaps I will go and lie down.

MISS PRESTWOOD : That's very sensible. Let me help you. (She helps LAURA up)

GRAHAM (heartily): That's the drill. Get a good spot of the old shut-eye and you'll be as good as new in the morning.

HOWARD : You said that before.

GRAHAM : Oh. Did I? (As LAURA turns upstage she sees the girl in the red coat. The latter gazes back at her for some moments, then turns and, still expressionless, exits R., not hurriedly)

LAURA : Who was that?

GRAHAM (who is upstage): Where? (He looks out through french window) Oh, that's Annette Fielding.

LAURA : I've seen her before.

GRAHAM : Oh no. No, you can't have.

HOWARD : Why can't she?

GRAHAM : Well, old boy, according to what Miss Prestwood told us, Miss Harrington's been living in Dublin for a couple of years.

HOWARD : She could have seen her before she went to Dublin,

couldn't she?

GRAHAM : Oh. Never thought of that.

LAURA : No. I've seen her not very long ago . . . I think. But I can't remember where. *(She puts her hand to her forehead)*

MISS PRESTWOOD : Is your head aching?

LAURA : Yes, a little.

MISS PRESTWOOD : I'll get you some aspirin. Now come along and we'll soon have you tucked up. Let me have your coat. *(She helps LAURA off with her coat)* There we are.

LAURA : I wish I could remember where I'd seen that girl before.

GRAHAM : Goodnight, Miss Harrington. Hope you sleep well.

HOWARD : Goodnight.

MISS PRESTWOOD : I've put you in a downstairs room, dear. It's Miss Lorrimer's old suite. Just along the passage.

LAURA : Thank you. *(She exits U.L., followed by MISS PRESTWOOD)*

GRAHAM : Looks a bit done up, doesn't she? Nasty business, fainting like that. *(He stops as he sees HOWARD is pacing slowly towards ENTR. L., clearly very thoughtful about LAURA)* Something the matter, old boy?

HOWARD : Mm? Oh no. Now — where's my perishing basket?

GRAHAM : How's it going, old boy?

HOWARD *(picking up the basket):* Just about the right size for stuffing over the ears of anybody who tries to get funny about it.

GRAHAM : No need to be touchy, old man. *(HOWARD sits and tosses the basket on to the table in front of him. ANNETTE FIELDING enters D.R., still wearing her red coat)* Hallo, Annette. What have you been doing with yourself?

ANNETTE : Just walking.

GRAHAM : Oh. Well, nice evening for it.

ANNETTE : We arranged to walk down to the village and meet Miss Harrington's train. Remember?

GRAHAM : Oh . . . Well, we didn't actually fix it, did we?

HOWARD : Yes. I heard you fix it.

GRAHAM *(uncomfortably):* What I said was we *might* go and meet Miss Harrington's train, if I remember right.

HOWARD : You *don't* remember right, mate.

GRAHAM *(to ANNETTE):* At the last moment something came up.

ANNETTE : Yes. You were going with Elsa, weren't you? *(As GRAHAM is about to protest)* Oh, never mind . . . So Miss Harrington got here all right, then?

GRAHAM : Yes. She's not feeling too fit after the journey, so Miss P's taken her off to bed.

ANNETTE : Pity. It would have put the evening in nicely to have somebody new to talk to. *(Going L.)* That means television, I suppose. *(Stops and looks back, not very hopefully, at GRAHAM)* Unless you'd still like to go for that walk. *(HOWARD picks at his basket)*

GRAHAM : Well, I'd like to, Annette, only—

HOWARD : Only he knows darn well that Elsa won't let him off the leash.

GRAHAM : Look, Carson, I do wish you'd mind your own business. (ANNETTE *goes to* ENTR. U.L.)

ANNETTE : By the way, we've got a visitor.

GRAHAM : Oh, Who is it?

HOWARD : Not another customer, poor devil?

ANNETTE : It's a man. I saw him get out of a taxi at the front gate and the porter sent him up the drive. *(To* GRAHAM—*)* Sure you won't change your mind about a walk, Graham?

GRAHAM : Perhaps tomorrow. (ANNETTE *is silent for some moments then gives a resigned little nod and exits* U.L.) Wonder who this bod is. Miss P. didn't say anything about anybody new coming, did she?

HOWARD : Not as far as I know. (MILLIE *enters* U.L., *pulling on her coat)* Where are you going?

MILLIE : Now that Miss Harrington's goin' off to bed Maggie Prestwood says I can go. Look after this geezer, will you, Mr Carson?

HOWARD : Which geezer?

MILLIE : I dunno who he is. I've told Miss Prestwood — she'll be down in a minute. *(Going to french window)* I'm off before she changes her mind about lettin' me go. 'Night-night apiece. *(She hurries out* OFF R. DETECTIVE-INSPECTOR KERSHAW *enters* U.L., *strolling in at a leisurely pace. He wears dark clothes and is quite a fatherly figure—affable, in a quiet, deliberate way and he usually wears a genial smile even when he is putting probing questions)*

KERSHAW *(smiling affably)*: Good evening.

GRAHAM : Oh, hallo, there. Come right in. Are you — ?

KERSHAW : Yes, I'm the geezer she was talking about.

GRAHAM *(in some confusion)*: Sorry about that. She didn't mean anything — you know —

KERSHAW : Oh, that's all right. I've been called a lot worse than that. *(Chuckles)* Yes, indeed.

GRAHAM : Well, Miss Prestwood'll be down in a minute. (KERSHAW *nods, beaming)* Won't you sit down?

KERSHAW : No, no. I'll stand, if you don't mind. Been travelling most of the day, you know, and it's a relief to stretch my legs.

HOWARD : Oh? . . . Is Miss Prestwood expecting you?

KERSHAW : No, no. Oh no.

HOWARD : Oh. Well, my name's Carson.

GRAHAM : And mine's Peters. (KERSHAW *nods, genial as ever)*

KERSHAW : Nice situation for a Convalescent Home, right in the country, secluded, lovely trees. A wee bit isolated, though. No staff problems?

HOWARD : No. No staff, either.

GRAHAM : Don't take him too literally, Mr — er — *(He pauses for* KERSHAW *to supply the name, but* KERSHAW *merely smiles)* We've a maid who lives in — the one you saw — and we have a couple of part-timers from the village — a cook and a waitress.

KERSHAW : Ah, not many patients, then?

GRAHAM : Only a handful of us just now. Actually, the place nearly closed down. The previous matron had a stroke or something and Miss Prestwood was only just able to keep things going.

KERSHAW : I see, I see . . . Oh, my name's Kershaw, by the way.

HOWARD : Do you know these parts, Mr Kershaw?

KERSHAW : Never been here in my life. No, I'm from the Smoke, as a lot of my clients call it.

HOWARD : Oh? I wouldn't have taken you for a Londoner.

KERSHAW : Oh, I wasn't *born* in London. Oh, no, no, no.

HOWARD : You just work there.

KERSHAW : W-e-l-l, yes and no.

HOWARD (*nods*): Yes and no.

KERSHAW : Or as you might say, here and there.

HOWARD (*nods again*): Here and there. (KERSHAW *smiles agreement*) Well, now we've got that sorted out we can relax. (*He sits back in his chair.* ELSA *enters U.L.*)

GRAHAM : Oh, Elsa — this is Mr Kershaw. He wants to see Miss Prestwood . . . I think.

ELSA : Yes, I heard Millie telling her. (*To* KERSHAW—) She's coming now.

KERSHAW : Thank you, thank you.

GRAHAM : This is Miss Milburn.

KERSHAW : How d'you do, Miss Milburn?

ELSA : Are you here to join us, Mr Kershaw?

KERSHAW : Join you? Oh, you mean for convalescence. (*Laughs*) Oh, no, no, no. I can't afford to be ill. At least not in an expensive establishment like this. No, I'm just here on business.

ELSA : Oh, I see. (MISS PRESTWOOD *enters U.L.*) This is Miss Prestwood.

KERSHAW (*beaming on* MISS PRESTWOOD): Ah, good evening, ma'am.

MISS PRESTWOOD : Good evening. So sorry to have kept you waiting. You're the gentleman who wanted to see me?

ELSA : Miss Prestwood, this is Mr Kershaw.

KERSHAW : Detective-Inspector Kershaw.

HOWARD ⎫ What?
GRAHAM ⎬ (*all together*): Eh?
ELSA ⎭ Detective-Inspector?

KERSHAW : New Scotland Yard.

HOWARD (*incredulously*): Scotland Yard? (KERSHAW *turns in his deliberate way and looks at* HOWARD)

KERSHAW (*mildly*): That's right, sir.

HOWARD : But — but — Scotland Yard!

KERSHAW (*handing* HOWARD *his opened wallet*): Would you care to look at my warrant-card, sir?

GRAHAM (*looking over* HOWARD'S *shoulder at the wallet*): He is, you know.

HOWARD : How right you are. (KERSHAW *pockets his wallet*)

MISS PRESTWOOD (*a little flustered*): I really can't think what Scotland Yard can want with our little Convalescent Home—

KERSHAW : I believe you've got a Miss Harrington staying with you.

MISS PRESTWOOD : Yes, that's right. She arrived a short time ago.

KERSHAW : Could I have a word with her?

MISS PRESTWOOD: Well, she's just going to bed. She's not very well.

KERSHAW : Really, now. I'm sorry to hear it. Nothing serious, I hope?

MISS PRESTWOOD : Well, she fainted twice today on the journey.

KERSHAW (*sympathetically*): Now isn't that too bad? Leaves you very weak and shaky, fainting does. Yes. Poor girl. Still, I won't keep her more than a few minutes, Miss Prestwood.

MISS PRESTWOOD : I'm sorry, Inspector. I'm afraid not.

KERSHAW : It would save me having to call back again in the morning, you see. I don't want to have to stay overnight in the village if I can help it.

MISS PRESTWOOD (*doubtfully*): Well, I don't know— (LAURA *enters U.L. her handbag over her arm*)

LAURA : I left my case in here—

MISS PRESTWOOD : Oh— we were just talking about you, Miss Harrington.

LAURA : Oh, were you? Now, where did I leave it?. Oh yes—over there. (*Laying her handbag aside, she goes for her case*)

ELSA : Laura, this gentleman is here to see you. He's from the police. (LAURA *stops dead*)

LAURA : The . . . police? (KERSHAW *comes slowly to her, smiling genially*)

KERSHAW : Good evening, Miss Harrington. I'm Detective-Inspector Kershaw, New Scotland Yard. (LAURA *has had a shock. Putting her case on the floor she gazes at* KERSHAW *as though hypnotised*)

LAURA : What . . . what do you want?

KERSHAW (*pleasantly*): I understand you crossed by boat from Ireland this morning—Waterford to Fishguard.

LAURA (*covering up her tenseness*): Yes.

KERSHAW : From Fishguard you went by train to London— Paddington Station.

LAURA : Yes.

KERSHAW : Then, of course, from Paddington to here, having changed trains at two connections on the way. Did you break your journey at all?

LAURA : No.

KERSHAW : Did you meet anyone on the way?

LAURA : No. No-one. (KERSHAW'S *genial manner vanishes*)

KERSHAW (*keenly*): Did anybody try to contact you?

LAURA : No.

KERSHAW (*the same*): Think carefully, Miss Harrington. This is important. Did anybody approach you and ask you to deliver a package, say? Or even a message?

LAURA : No. I didn't speak to anybody—except porters, people like that. (*She is in a state of tension*)

KERSHAW : Oh. (*He eyes* LAURA *searchingly for some moments.*

Then he relaxes and beams genially on her) Well, that clears that up. *(He turns away and gets out pipe and pouch)*

LAURA : Is that all? . . . Is that all you wanted to see me about?

KRESHAW *(turning back to her)*: Did you think there might be something more?

LAURA : No . . . No, of course not. *(She is seen almost to go limp with relief)* How — how did you know I was here?

KERSHAW *(consulting notebook)*: Let's see now. *(Reads—)* " Information from Dublin Constabulary." I suppose you left word at your old address that any letters were to be sent on to you here?

LAURA : Yes, I did.

KERSHAW : Then I expect the Dublin police called there.

LAURA : Yes, of course. But—

KERSHAW *(genially)*: They asked us to make a routine check in connection with a matter they're investigating but it's clear you know nothing about it. No need for you to worry, Miss Harrington.

MISS PRESTWOOD *(fussily)*: There! All finished. Now you can run along to your room.

LAURA : Yes. Yes, I'll do that. *(She makes for* ENTR. U.L.*)*

KERSHAW *(filling his pipe)*: Oh, Miss Harrington. There was one more thing. *(*LAURA *stops and freezes, not turning)*

LAURA : Yes?

KESRHAW : Would you happen to have your passport handy?

LAURA : My passport?

KERSHAW : Yes, I've got to jot down the details of it. Purely a matter of routine. You know—coming from Eire to take up residence in this country again, if our information is correct.

HOWARD : Do they send Detective-Inspectors to check on passports?

KERSHAW : You never can tell what my Superintendent is going to do, Mr Carson. *(Chuckles)* You'd be surprised at the jobs he gives me. Once sent me to arrest a woman who was known to be having a baby. If the landlady hadn't happened to come in I'd have had to be midwife. Well, Miss Harrington?

LAURA : Yes, I've got my passport with me. *(She is more at ease again)*

KERSHAW : Good, good. That means I'll be able to get back to London tonight. Very glad, too. That little inn down in the village—what is it? the "Black Bull?"—didn't look as though they make you very comfortable. *(Taking note-book and fountain pen from his pocket)* Now, Miss Prestwood—if there's somewhere I can do my bit of writing?

MISS PRESTWOOD : Yes, the writing-room's just along the passage. This way, Inspector. *(She exits* U.L.*)*

KERSHAW *(following, stops)*: I'll have to trouble you to fill in the details for me, Miss Harrington, so perhaps you'll bring your passport along.

LAURA : Yes, It's in my case. *(She goes for her case)* Oh, it's locked. *(Comes back to her handbag and takes out a key.* KERSHAW, *with* a genial nod, exits U.L.)

GRAHAM : Here you are. (He puts LAURA's case on the table)

LAURA : Thank you. (At the side or back of the table, so that she does not mask it from the audience, she unlocks her case and opens it, laying the lid right back. She is about to put her hand in when she sees something inside. She stares in horror then becomes faint, puts her hand over her eyes and sways)

ELSA : Laura! . . . Laura—is anything the matter? (GRAHAM is just in time to catch LAURA as she collapses. ELSA goes quickly to her) She's fainted again. You know, there must be something the matter with her.

HOWARD : This time it was from shock. Something she saw in her case. (He puts his hand in the case and brings out necklaces, bracelets and brooches, all of diamonds. They all gaze at them incredulously. Then—)

KERSHAW (OFF L.): Miss Harrington. (HOWARD looks from ELSA to GRAHAM, then is seen to take a decision. He puts the jewellery back into the case quickly, but deliberately and without panic)

ELSA : But— (HOWARD quickly gives her a look of warning, then a brief shake of the head. He shuts down the lid his manner all the time being serious but composed. KERSHAW enters U.L., followed by MISS PRESTWOOD)

KERSHAW : Miss Harrington, perhaps after all I needn't— (He sees LAURA) Oh dear. (GRAHAM puts LAURA in a chair. MISS PRESTWOOD goes to her. HOWARD slowly turns his back on LAURA and the others and remains facing front or towards DOWNSTAGE R., his hands resting on the closed lid of the case)

CURTAIN

END OF ACT ONE

ACT TWO

Scene I. NEXT MORNING

(At CURTAIN RISE morning sunlight is seen beyond the french window. MILLIE, carrying a Dustette vacuum-cleaner, duster, etc., is in the opening calling to OFF R.)

MILLIE: 'Morning', Fred . . . Nice mornin', isn't it? . . . (More loudly—) I said it's a nice mornin'. What's the matter with you —gone deaf or somethin'? You want to make old Thelma Transom an offer for one of her old hearin'-aids! . . . You'll what? You and who else? . . . (Squeals and scurries back) No — I'm only kiddin' (Laughs) You're still my favourite milkman . . . Cheerio Fred. See you in the mornin'. (She comes downstage and lays out her cleaning materials as MISS TRANSOM enters U.L., carrying the case of her transistor set, with the cord leading to the earphone which is in her ear)

MISS TRANSOM: I heard that—I heard that!

MILLIE: You 'eard what?

MISS TRANSOM: What you said about my hearing-aid and I won't have it!

MILLIE (indicating the transistor-set): Mate, you've got it! (She glances round cautiously) Here—did anythin' happen after I'd gone to the flicks last night? I've heard a few odds and ends, but—

MISS TRANSOM: Eh?

MILLIE: I said what happened after I'd gone to—

MISS TRANSOM (overlapping): I've gone deaf.

MILLIE: Gone deaf? You always were deaf!

MISS TRANSOM: What d'you say? (She bangs the set with her free hand)

MILLIE (loudly): What was goin' on last night?

MISS TRANSOM: I can't hear a thing. (Still banging) Ah, that's better. (MILLIE, filling her lung deeply, does not hear the last few words)

MILLIE (bawling): I SAID WHAT WAS GOIN' ON LAST NIGHT?

MISS TRANSOM: There's no need for you to shout. This hearing-aid is very powerful.

MILLIE (bitterly): Oh, mate!

MISS TRANSOM (gleefully): Oh, such excitement! Miss Harrington fainted and Mr Peters had to carry her to her bedroom. He's a detective from Scotland Yard, you know.

MILLIE (incredulously): What — Mr Peters?

MISS TRANSOM: No, no, no. That man you showed in just before you went off. (HOWARD appears in ENTR. U.L. He stays there, getting out cigarettes and lighter, unseen by the others)

MILLIE: Oh, you mean that tall geezer in the grey suit. (Alter as *necessary)*

MISS TRANSOM : Yes. *(Impressively—)* And he was asking Miss Harrington all sorts of questions.

HOWARD : How do you know? *(He strolls in)*

MISS TRANSOM *(jumps)*: Oh! Mr Carson—how you startled me . . . Now I've gone off the air again. *(Bangs her receiver)* It's no use —I'll have to get another hearing-aid.

MILLIE : Why, you've got six already.

HOWARD : I expect it's only a bad connection. Here let me see it. *(He pinches where the cord joins the receiver)* How's that?

MISS TRANSOM : Wonderful! I must bring you my other five aids to mend.

HOWARD : How did you know that Scotland Yard man was questioning Miss Harrington? You weren't even in the room.

MISS TRANSOM *(cunningly)*: I don't need to be in a room to know what's going on in it . . . *(Pats her receiver)* thanks to my hearing-aid.

HOWARD *(nods)*: I get it. You were along the passage there, listening in.

MISS TRANSOM : Yes, but I could have heard just as well if I'd been on the other side of that closed door. *(Indicating DOOR R.)*

MILLIE : Well, I don't believe that, for a start!

MISS TRANSOM : There's a lot of things you don't know about, young woman. *(Going R.)* Well, I mustn't stand here gossiping. I have to go and cut some dahlias for Miss Milburn to arrange in the vases. Excuse me. *(She exits R.)*

MILLIE : You know, if you ask me, she hasn't got all her marbles.

HOWARD : Ssh! . . . *(Brief silence while he looks at DOOR R. Then he speaks deliberately—)* Mary had a little lamb, it's fleece was white as snow. *(MILLIE gapes at him. He goes to DOOR R.)* And everywhere that Mary went . . . *(He pulls the door open. MISS TRANSOM is holding up her receiver in a position where it would have been pressed against the door)*

MISS TRANSOM *(triumphantly)*: The lamb was sure to go.

MILLIE : You *could* hear through that door!

MISS TRANSOM : I told you I could. You see, all I have to do is turn it up to full volume. Then I could even hear a whisper.

MILLIE : Coo, we'll have to watch it when you're around won't we? *(MISS TRANSOM gives her witch-like chuckle)*

MISS TRANSOM : See you later. *(She disappears and HOWARD shuts the door. MILLIE goes L., taking her cleaning materials)*

MILLIE : Is Miss Harrington okay again this mornin', then?

HOWARD : I think so. She had her breakfast in her room, so I haven't seen her but Miss Prestwood says she's all right.

MILLIE : Oh. Well, we'll be seein' what's what then, won't we?

HOWARD : I expect so.

MILLIE : Well, back to the forced labour. *(She exits U.L. HOWARD stands looking thoughtful for some time, then slowly goes up-stage. He gazes unseeingly through french window to OFF R. as he lights a cigarette. ELSA enters U.L., followed by GRAHAM)*

ELSA : There you are, Howard. Have you seen Laura?

HOWARD : Not yet.

ELSA : Howard, we've got to do something about that jewellery.

HOWARD : We are doing something about it—holding on to it until
we hear what Miss Laura Harrington's got to say. Isn't that what
we agreed last night?

GRAHAM : I don't know so much about agreed. You seemed to take
the whole matter into your own hands.

HOWARD : Okay, so I took it into my own hands.

GRAHAM : Those diamonds must be worth a fortune—if they're real,
of course.

HOWARD : Real? They're worth fifty or sixty thousand pounds.

GRAHAM : What! (HOWARD *realizes he has made a slip*)

ELSA (*curiously*): How would you know, Howard? . . .Oh, of course,
you're in the underwriting business, aren't you? (*Neither she nor*
GRAHAM *notes* HOWARD'S *relief*)

GRAHAM : Well, I don't like the responsibility of holding them.

HOWARD (*drily*): You aren't holding them. I am.

ELSA : But we're all involved. Miss Prestwood as well, now.

HOWARD (*to* GRAHAM): I still can't understand why you had to go
and tell her about finding those diamonds.

GRAHAM : Well, she *is* in charge here. It seemed only right to put
her in the picture.

ELSA : Aren't we all accessories or something, if the diamonds are
stolen?

GRAHAM : If? Of course they're stolen—they must be.

HOWARD (*to* ELSA): Do you think Laura Harrington stole them?

ELSA : Don't be ridiculous. Of course she didn't.

HOWARD : Then don't you think we ought to hear what she has to
say before we start making trouble for her with Kershaw? She
may have a perfectly good answer—the jewellery may not even
be stolen.

ELSA : Yes. Yes, Howard, perhaps you're right. (MISS PRESTWOOD
enters U.L.) Is Laura up yet?

MISS PRESTWOOD : Yes, she's coming now. Oh dear, what a night I
had. I scarcely slept a wink, thinking about all that jewellery in
the house.

ELSA : But you haven't said anything to Laura about it?

MISS PRESTWOOD : Not a word. We agreed not to worry her.

ELSA : I'm sure she'll be able to clear everything up when we talk
to her.

MISS PRESTWOOD : Here she is. (*They look towards* ENTR. U.L.
Brief wait, then LAURA *enters. She is composed but quiet*)

GRAHAM (*heartily*): Ah, good morning, Miss Harrington.

HOWARD : Good morning.

LAURA : Good morning.

ELSA (*putting her arm round* LAURA): Laura, darling—come and sit
down.

LAURA : I'm perfectly all right, Elsa.

GRAHAM : Did you have a good night's sleep?

LAURA : Yes. Miss Prestwood gave me a tablet. (She sits)

GRAHAM : Jolly good. Well now, if you feel up to it, we thought
. . . well, you know—we felt a little chat might be a good idea.

HOWARD : He means—what about that jewellery in your case?

ELSA : Howard, you needn't be quite so blunt.

HOWARD : I think Miss Harrington would prefer it to a lot of shilly-
shallying.

LAURA : Yes, I would.

HOWARD : The jewellery isn't yours?

LAURA : No. No, it isn't mine. And I haven't the faintest idea how
it got into my case.

ELSA : There. I was sure Laura would say she knows nothing about
the jewellery. Now we know what to do.

LAURA : What to do?

ELSA : Yes. Hand it over to Kershaw and that's the end of it.
(LAURA looks away, a strained expression on her face)

MISS PRESTWOOD (pleased): Yes. If you remember, that's what I
wanted to do last night. Oh, I'll be so relieved to be rid of such
valuable property. (MILLIE enters U.L.)

MILLIE : Miss Prestwood, Cook said to ask you about Miss
Transom's diet.

MISS PRESTWOOD : Not now, Millie, I'm busy.

MILLIE : Or perhaps I ought to be askin' Miss Harrington now.

MISS PRESTWOOD : I suppose I'd better go and see to it. (She exits
U.L.)

MILLIE : I know what diet the old faggot would get from me!
(She exits U.L. LAURA's strained look is still there as her eyes
follow MILLIE)

LAURA : What did she mean about asking me?

HOWARD : Well, it is your department, isn't it? (LAURA looks at him
quickly, half afraid, half-puzzled)

ELSA : Look — Inspector Kershaw said he would be here about
ten o'clock. We haven't much time.

GRAHAM : No. Let's get down to business. Now, Laura (He laughs)
I hope that's okay — Elsa's talked about you so much we've got
into the habit of calling you Laura—you say you know nothing
about how those diamonds got into your case.

LAURA : Nothing whatever.

GRAHAM : Did you pack it yourself?

LAURA : Yes.

GRAHAM : Lock it?

LAURA : Yes.

GRAHAM : And after that it was never out of your possession?

LAURA : No, never . . . Except—

HOWARD (nods): Except when you fainted, Right?

LAURA : Yes. Yes, that's right. I've been thinking about that. I
don't think I just fainted.

ELSA : What do you mean, Laura?

HOWARD : She could have been doped.

GRAHAM : Doped?

LAURA : That could account for why I fainted again when I got here last night—tired after a long journey, hungry. There are one or two drugs which could produce that effect a number of hours later if you were allergic to them.

HOWARD : Did you have anything to drink on board?

LAURA : Yes. Yes, I did. A stewardess brought me a cup of coffee just as we were getting in at Fishguard.

HOWARD : Had you ordered it?

LAURA : No. She said it was part of the service.

HOWARD : Funny time to bring coffee round. Had you seen that stewardess before?

LAURA : No. No, I hadn't.

GRAHAM : You mean the stewardess was phoney?

HOWARD (shrugs): Could be. The uniform would be easy enough. Let's say, for a starting-point, that that was when the jewellery was planted in Miss Harrington's case. Now—

GRAHAM (overlapping): But her case was locked—she said so.

HOWARD : And where would she put the key?

GRAHAM : What? Well, in her handbag, I suppose.

HOWARD : And if you could think of that, don't you think somebody else could?

GRAHAM : Well, if you put it like that—yes, I suppose they could.

ELSA : But who would want to? And why?

HOWARD : Try this one for size. Somebody wants to get a load of hot diamonds out of Eire into England. They could be scared they're being watched at the port by the police—so they plant them on somebody who has a clean passport—somebody quite above suspicion.

GRAHAM : But — but that's all surmise.

HOWARD : It's called building a theory that could fit the facts. That's what they train Scotland Yard detectives to do.

LAURA : But whoever put the diamonds in my case . . . they'd want to get them back.

HOWARD (nods): Right. They'll want to get them back.

ELSA : You mean they'll . . . Laura, this leaves you no choice. You've got to tell Inspector Kershaw.

LAURA : No.

ELSA : But you must!

LAURA (vehemently): No, I tell you! He mustn't know about it!

ELSA : Then what are you going to do?

LAURA : I— (She hesitates, then helplessly—) I don't know.

ELSA : I simply can't understand what you're afraid of.

HOWARD : Think again, Elsa.

ELSA : What d'you mean?

HOWARD : If she says to Kershaw 'Here's a lot of jewellery. I found it in my case but I don't know anything about it'—do you think Kershaw will say 'Oh, thanks very much' and leave it at that?

GRAHAM : You mean he'll suspect Laura of having stolen it.

ELSA : But they couldn't prove anything against her.

HOWARD : She's in possession of stolen property and she can't give a satisfactory explanation of how she came by it. You know what Kershaw will write in his Report Sheet on that one? 'I accordingly took the prisoner into custody pending further enquiries being made.'

LAURA (*tensely*): No, no, no!

ELSA : Do you think Inspector Kershaw's here about the jewellery?

HOWARD : That's what I'd like to know. Until we do, we sit tight and say nothing.

GRAHAM : But listen, old boy—

HOWARD : We say nothing.

LAURA (*desperately*): Please, Elsa. (GRAHAM *and* ELSA *look at each other in silence. Then*—)

ELSA (*smiles*): All right, darling. (*She pats* LAURA's *hand comfortingly*) We'll keep it to ourselves. Well, now I'd better get along and arrange the flowers, if Miss Transom's got them in. (*To* LAURA—) Miss Prestwood has little jobs for all of us . . . Don't worry—I'm sure everything will turn out all right. (LAURA *returns her smile and* ELSA *exits U.L.*)

GRAHAM (*breezily*): Well now—how about a nice walk in the grounds until Kershaw shows up? (ANNETTE *appears from* OFF R.) We've got some lovely old beech trees and nice flowering shrubs, haven't we, old boy?

LAURA : Some other time, thank you.

GRAHAM : Do you good, you know. Put the roses back in your cheeks and all that.

LAURA (*smiles her thanks*): I'd like to stay here and relax just now.

GRAHAM : Just as you say.

ANNETTE (*coming downstage*): You should have taken Graham up on his invitation while you had the chance, Miss Harrington. (GRAHAM *looks slightly annoyed rather than put out*) After a time, he isn't too free with his invitations. I ought to know.

GRAHAM : Annette, Miss Harrington doesn't want to listen to—

ANNETTE (*overlapping*): No, of course she doesn't. Well, Graham?

GRAHAM (*resignedly*): Come along, then. (ANNETTE *exits by french window, followed by* GRAHAM)

LAURA : I do wish I could remember where I've seen her before.

HOWARD : Didn't you say something about wanting to relax? (*He offers her a cigarette but she smiles and shakes her head*)

LAURA : Yes, I did.

HOWARD : Well, you won't do it if you go on worrying about where you've seen Annette.

LAURA (*smiles again*): Actually, I do feel relaxed—a little. I can't imagine why, after all yesterday's excitement.

HOWARD : Good.

LAURA : You seem different this morning, too.

HOWARD : Oh. Do I?

LAURA : Yes. I didn't like you a bit last night. In fact, I thought you were quite horrid.

HOWARD : Yes — I thought I was, too. One of my off days. All part of my complaint, you know.

LAURA : And what is your complaint?

HOWARD : Well, you'll know the quacks' jargon for it but, in non-medical language, the screaming hab-dabs.

LAURA (impatiently): Why does everybody keep talking as though I should know all about their illnesses and treatment and things?

HOWARD : It would be too bad if you didn't. Elsa's given you quite a build-up, you know.

LAURA (surprised): Oh? I can't think why she should. We've never seen or heard anything of each other since we left school.

HOWARD : No, but . . . (A thought strikes him) What about your letters, then?

LAURA : What letters?

HOWARD : The ones that passed between you about coming here.

LAURA (bewildered): I don't know what you're talking about. (HOWARD seems about to pursue the subject further, then gives a slight shrug. MILLIE enters U.L.)

MILLIE (indignantly): Here — do you know what?

HOWARD : What?

MILLIE : The police is here!

HOWARD : Kershaw?

MILLIE : Yes. He's talkin' to Miss Prestwood. Wants to see everybody, he does. Even me and Cook.

LAURA : Did he say why he was here?

MILLIE : Not to me, he didn't. He's talkin' to Miss Prestwood now. But if he starts askin' me questions I'll tell him I don't say nothin' unless me lawyer's present.

HOWARD : Why?

MILLIE : I dunno. But I know it's the clever thing to do, 'cos I've seen it on the telly. (Going L. stops) Oh, I came to tell you not to go out until Inspector What's-his-name's seen you. A right old carry-on, ain't it? Next thing you know, you'll 'ave to put your hand up to ask if you can leave the room. (She exits U.L. HOWARD notices that LAURA is worried)

HOWARD : Worried about Kershaw?

LAURA : No. (Almost angrily) No — why should I be? (She paces upstage) What . . . what have you done with the jewellery?

HOWARD : It's safe.

LAURA : Why did the others let you have it?

HOWARD : They didn't. I took it.

LAURA : Why?

HOWARD: Why? (He considers this. Then—) I don't know actually. It just seemed a good idea. (LAURA looks at him, half-fearful, half-hopefully, trying to read him. ANNETTE and GRAHAM enter by french window. LAURA sits)

ANNETTE : Miss Prestwood says that police inspector wants to see us all.

HOWARD : That's right.

ANNETTE : What does he want?

HOWARD : Stick around and we'll all find out. (ELSA enters U.L.)

ELSA : Where've you been, Graham?

ANNETTE : Only in the garden. What's the matter? Getting worried because he was out of your sight for five minutes? We were only talking about those diamonds being found in Miss Harrington's case.

HOWARD (to GRAHAM): Have you been shooting off your month?

GRAHAM : No! . . . Well, I — well, Annette caught something when Miss Prestwood was telling me about Kershaw wanting to see us all. I had to tell her the rest.

HOWARD : There's no 'had to' about it! Did you tell Miss Transom too?

GRAHAM : No, I didn't! . . . But I'll bet she knows, all the same. She finds out about everything. She not only *looks* like a witch —I sometimes think she is one.

ELSA : Oh, I'll be glad when all this business is over.

ANNETTE (looking L.): They're coming now.

MISS PRESTWOOD (OFF L.): This way, Inspector. (KERSHAW carrying his notebook, enters U.L., followed by MISS PRESTWOOD)

KERSHAW (genially): Good morning, ladies and gentlemen. Beautiful morning. It's a real treat to be working out of London on a day like this, I can tell you . . . Well, Miss Harrington, and how are you feeling this morning?

LAURA : Perfectly all right, Inspector.

KERSHAW : And very glad I am to hear it. Miss Prestwood was telling me about the trying time you had yesterday. Very unfortunate. I'd have liked to have left you alone a bit longer but I have a job to so—so the sooner I get on with it the sooner you'll be rid of me.

HOWARD : What's it all about, Inspector?

KERSHAW (folding back his notebook): I'm coming to it, Mr Carson. (Smiling) You young folk are always in a hurry. Now, I've got to the age where I like to take my time over things. I find by jogging comfortably along I get there just as quickly in the end.

HOWARD : But why all of us—all here together, I mean?

KERSHAW : Because I want your help in a matter I'm investigating and by getting you all together I'll only have to explain it once.

HOWARD : I see. Okay.

KERSHAW : Now then. Miss Prestwood's been able to give me the background of all of you. All of you, that is, except . . .

LAURA : Except me. Isn't that what you were going to say?

KERSHAW (smiles genially): Well, perhaps we can get that sorted out, Miss Harrington. Now Miss Prestwood told me about you coming from Dublin to take up your position here but that's about all, so perhaps you'll be kind enough to tell me a little more.

LAURA (guardedly): What do you want to know?

KERSHAW : You've been living in Dublin for some time, I understand.

LAURA : Yes.

KERSHAW : Might I ask how long?

LAURA : Two years.

KERSHAW (*looking at notebook*): Two years . . . You'd be working, of course.

LAURA : Yes. I was in private employment. (KERSHAW *looks at her enquiringly and waits for her to continue. Unwillingly, she adds*—) To . . . to a man who was a diabetic.

KERSHAW (*nods*): Ah, private nursing.

LAURA : No! (*Checks herself, More quietly*—) No. I was his personal secretary.

KERSHAW : Secretary? But . . . (*He looks at his notes again, then gives a slight shrug*) What was your employer's profession, Miss Harrington ?

LAURA : He . . . he was retired

KERSHAW : Retired, eh ? A man of means, no doubt ?

LAURA : I . . . yes, I suppose so. But with his health being so bad he always had to have somebody around.

KERSHAW : Ah, money can't buy good health, can it ? Sometimes I meet wealthy men in my job — fat expense accounts, country houses and so on. Then I see them nursing their stomach ulcers and I think to myself — "Well, Tom, old lad, a policeman's pay isn't a fortune but by George you've got your health and that's what matters."

LAURA (*the strain getting too much for her*) : Inspector, for goodness' sake —

KERSHAW (*mildly*) : Yes, Miss Harrington ?

LAURA (*controlling herself with an effort*) : I'm sorry.

KERSHAW : No, no, no — I'm the one who should apologize — rambling on like that. Now — (*Turning back a page of his notebook*) — about you coming to take up your position at Abbot's Mead. Where are we? You know, my writing's so bad I can hardly read it myself.

LAURA : Have you got things about me in that book ?

KERSHAW : Mm ? Oh, I've had everybody's background from Miss Prestwood, you know . . . Ah, here we are. Yes, there was an advertisement, and then you —

LAURA : What advertisement ?

KERSHAW : In the medical journals — about Abbot's Mead.

LAURA : I don't know anything about any advertisement. (ELSA and MISS PRESTWOOD *look at each other in surprise* GRAHAM *also looks puzzled*).

KERSHAW : I mean the one that invited applications for the position here.

LAURA : And I tell you I know nothing about it. (KERSHAW *glances at* MISS PRESTWOOD, *who gives a bewildered shake of the head. He turns deliberately back to* LAURA)

KERSHAW : Then how did you know there was a vacancy here, Miss Harrington?

LAURA (*evasively*) : Well, I — someone told me.

KERSHAW : Who told you ?

LAURA : It was — it was a woman who came from around here somewhere. She was on holiday in Dublin.

KERSHAW : Someone you knew ?

LAURA : No, no. I was having a cup of tea in a cafe in O'Connell Street and she came and sat at my table. We got talking and she told me of a job going in a convalescent home in the country that had been allowed to run down.

MISS PRESTWOOD : I explained about that to you, Inspector. Miss Lorrimer was the previous owner but her health began to fail and she let things go. We actually got to the stage where there was only one guest here — Miss Transom.

KERSHAW (*nodding genially*) : No wonder you wanted some fresh blood, eh, Miss Prestwood ?

MISS PRESTWOOD : Yes, indeed. Then poor Miss Lorrimer had a severe stroke and they had to take her away. I did my best to carry on for the time being and we picked up a little — six or seven guests, that sort of average — but after all I'm not qualified. I was very glad when Miss Harrington agreed to come, I can tell you.

LAURA : What do you mean, agreed to come?

MISS PRESTWOOD : Well, you—

LAURA (*overlapping*): I wrote to you, asking if it was true about the vacancy, we exchanged a few letters and finally you gave me the job.

KERSHAW : Job? (HOWARD, GRAHAM, ANNETTE *and* ELSA *react in astonishment*) You did say job?

LAURA : Yes, I did.

ELSA   ⎫ (*together*)   Laura, what are you saying? (*Etc., ad lib*).
GRAHAM ⎰   Miss Prestwood gave you a job? (*Etc.*)

KERSHAW (*overlapping*): Just a minute, if you don't mind. (*They subside.* KERSHAW *speaks very deliberately*) Miss Harrington, will you please tell me what position you came to Abbot's Mead to take up?

LAURA : Hasn't Miss Prestwood told you?

KERSHAW : I want you to tell me.

LAURA : I came here as receptionist. (*All but* KERSHAW *react in astonishment*)

HOWARD   ⎫ (*together*) :   As what?
ANNETTE ⎰   Receptionist? Oh, no!

ELSA (*overlapping*): Laura, you know that's not true.

GRAHAM (*overlapping*): You're joking — you must be.

KERSHAW (*overlapping*): Please — please! Miss Harrington, I think I ought to tell you that some of the statements you've just made do not agree with what I've got there.

LAURA : I can't help that. I've told you the truth. (*She is both alarmed and angry*) I can prove it. I've got all the correspondence I had with Miss Prestwood. (*She searches in her handbag*)

MISS PRESTWOOD (*gently, but in a rather worried tone*): But, Miss Harrington—that's impossible—

LAURA : She asked me to keep it and bring it with me for identific- ation. Here you are. (*She gives* KERSHAW *some letters which are clipped together at one corner*) Miss Prestwood's actual letters to me and the carbons of my replies to her.

MISS PRESTWOOD (*blankly*): But I didn't write you any letters.

LAURA: You didn't what?

MISS PRESTWOOD: All the business side of it was done by Mr Wetherburn.

KERSHAW (*reading and turning over the letters*): Who's Mr Wetherburn?

MISS PRESTWOOD: He's the agent who acted on behalf of Miss Lorrimer in the transfer. (KERSHAW *nods, still reading*) He interviewed Miss Harrington in Dublin.

LAURA: Interviewed me?

MISS PRESTWOOD: Miss Lorrimer's in Cornwall now, completely paralysed, so she couldn't interview her. I might have done so myself but with Miss Milburn having spoken so highly of her I didn't really think it was necessary.

LAURA: Elsa?

ELSA: I was only too glad to do it, darling.

LAURA (*pacing across the room in bewilderment*): This isn't happening. It can't be real! (KERSHAW *goes on reading the letters. He does not look up when* LAURA *goes to him*) Look—I don't know anything about an advertisement. I don't know anything about this man who's supposed to have interviewed me in Dublin. I tell you I first heard about Abbot's Mead from that woman I met in the cafe. You've got to believe me.

GRAHAM: Inspector, couldn't you let Miss Harrington off the hook for a bit? After all, she *did* get quite a crack on the head yesterday, you know.

KERSHAW (*looks up suddenly*): Ah yes. I was forgetting about the head injury. (*Something in the way he looks at her gives* LAURA *a sudden chill of fear. She looks round at the others;* ELSA *and* MISS PRESTWOOD *are looking at her in concern, the others in curiosity*)

LAURA: What . . what are you looking at me like that for?

MISS PRESTWOOD: Inspector, I warned you this might happen. (KERSHAW *nods and closes his notebook*)

LAURA: What might happen? (*Nobody answers. She goes to* MISS PRESTWOOD) What might happen?

KERSHAW: Well, we'll leave it at that for the present. Perhaps you'd like to go and get some rest, Miss Harrington.

LAURA: No, I wouldn't, thank you. I'd rather—

ANNETTE (*overlapping, getting up*): Can we go now?

KERSHAW: Yes, Miss Fielding. That's all for just now. (ANNETTE *moves towards* DOOR R.)

LAURA (*suddenly*): That girl! (ANNETTE *stops.* LAURA *goes quickly to her*) I've remembered where I've seen you before! Inspector —I told you about meeting a woman in a cafe in O'Connell Street, Dublin—the woman who told me about Abbot's Mead?

KERSHAW : Yes.

LAURA : Well, while we were talking I noticed a girl outside looking through the window. She seemed to be watching us. It was her! (*Dead silence. Then—*)

KERSHAW : Well, Miss Fielding?

ANNETTE (*very surprised*): I don't know what she's talking about.

LAURA : You know perfectly well. You were wearing a red coat and a white headscarf.

ANNETTE (*almost helplessly*): But I've never been in Dublin in my life.

LAURA : You're lying! (ANNETTE *tries to answer, but can do no more than give a little shrug of helplessness*)

KERSHAW : All right, thank you, Miss Fielding. (ANNETTE *exits by* DOOR R. LAURA *looks round and sees the looks of doubt*)

LAURA : Why won't anyone believe me?

ELSA : It isn't that, darling. It's . . .

LAURA : Well? (ELSA *gives a worried shake of the head*) Answer me!

MISS PRESTWOOD (*unwillingly*): Miss Harrington—the delayed effects of concussion can play strange tricks.

LAURA : Concussion! You mean I've lost my memory. That's what you mean, isn't it? (*Tensely—*) Isn't it?

ELSA : Well, if anyone should know, Laura — you should.

LAURA : *Why* should I? Why does everybody keep talking as though I should understand medical matters?

KERSHAW : Well, shouldn't you, Miss Harrington?

LAURA : No! I'm a secretary!

KERSHAW: But you haven't always been, have you, Miss Harrington?

LAURA : What are you getting at—why are you asking me all these questions?

KERSHAW : You said this was the correspondence that passed between you and Miss Prestwood, confirming your appointment as secretary/receptionist at Abbot's Mead?

LAURA : Yes. Yes, that's right. And those letters will prove that everything I've told you is true.

KERSHAW : They certainly prove *something*. The first one is a copy of a certificate which shows that you are a State Registered Nurse, trained at one of the principal London teaching hospitals. (LAURA *falls back with a gasp of dismay*). The others, Miss Harrington, establish beyond all doubt that you answered an advertisement in a medical journal saying that the lease of a convalescent home was for disposal to someone who was a State Registered Nurse. In one of the letters you give full particulars of your enrolment on the register of duly qualified nurses, in another is the acceptance of your application by the doctor and the lawyer acting for Miss Lorrimer, the previous matron. (*He has been turning the letters over. He stops at the last one and holds it out to* LAURA) Is that your signatuare?

LAURA : Yes. Yes, it is.

KERSHAW : This document is a copy of the transfer of the lease of the Convalescent Home to you. (*He folds the papers together without speaking for a moment. Then—*) Miss Harrington, you are the new proprietor of Abbot's Mead.

CURTAIN

END OF ACT TWO. SCENE 1.

ACT TWO

Scene 2. LATER THE SAME MORNING

(House-lights out. Stage lights up. The telephone-bell rings. Nobody answers it. The CURTAIN rises. The telephone goes on ringing. Presently it stops. In a few moments GRAHAM enters U.L., carrying his pipe. He goes to the 'phone and picks it up)

GRAHAM : Hallo . . . Hallo. *(Waits)* Hallo. *(Shrugs a little, then hangs up. He is slapping his pockets, searching for matches when ANNETTE enters U.L.)* Did you hear the telephone, Annette?

ANNETTE : No. *(She comes C., passing GRAHAM)*

GRAHAM : Oh. I thought I did, but there's no reply. Oh well, if it was anybody they'll ring again. *(He makes for ENTR. U.L.)*

ANNETTE : Don't go, Graham.

GRAHAM : 'Mm? *(Stops)*

ANNETTE : I'd like to talk to you.

GRAHAM *(unwillingly)*: Well — I —

ANNETTE : Why are you avoiding me, Graham?

GRAHAM : But I'm not. I mean—

ANNETTE *(overlapping)*: Yes you are. Whenever you find yourself alone with me you can't wait to get out of the room.

GRAHAM : Annette, you're imagining things.

ANNETTE : It wasn't like that once, was it?

GRAHAM : We were good friends, but — well, I —

ANNETTE : Good friends! Is that what you've told Elsa? Did you never tell her we were going to be married?

GRAHAM *(lamely)*: Well, nothing was actually settled, was it?

ANNETTE : Wasn't it? I thought it was.

GRAHAM : Look, Annette, I've really got to go. I've lots of things to do. *(Going L.)*

ANNETTE : Are you going to marry Elsa?

GRAHAM : Well, of all the things to—

ANNETTE : Are you?

GRAHAM : We've never even talked about it.

ANNETTE : Well, at least that's something, isn't it?

GRAHAM : Look, Annette, why don't you . . .

ANNETTE : Yes ?

GRAHAM : Oh . . . nothing. *(With a slight frown of annoyance he exits L., MILLIE, carrying a duster, enters R., in time to see him leave)*

MILLIE : Still havin' no luck, dear? *(Goes on dusting)*

ANNETTE : What do you mean by that?

MILLIE : You know what I mean, all right, ducks. With Mr Peters. Everybody knows you're stuck on him. But let's face it—you're up against pretty strong competition in Miss Milburn, aren't you?

ANNETTE *(furiously)*: How dare you talk about my affairs?

MILLIE: Got to talk about *somethin'*, ducks, or we'd all go off our trolley. (HOWARD *enters U.L., looking very preoccupied*)

HOWARD: Your turn, Annette.

ANNETTE: Inspector Kershaw?

HOWARD: Yes. He wants you now. (ANNETTE *exits U.L.* HOWARD *stands, frowning a little in thought, then lights a cigarette*)

MILLIE (*still dusting*): You had your session with the law then, Mr Carson?

HOWARD (*absently*): 'Mm? Oh — yes.

MILLIE: That Kershaw didn't get much change outa me, I can tell you. "I know all about you coppers," I sez to him, an' I do, too, 'Cos my cousin Freda's married to one. She sez they used to have big feet but now they're in the salary bracket they've got big mouths. So I sez to this Kershaw ha'porth, I sez, "I don't know what you want me for, I only work here. I don't know nothin' about nothin' an' if I did I wouldn't say nothin'. (MISS TRANSOM *enters U.L.*) Here she is—the Mad Witch of Abbot's Mead.

MISS TRANSOM: What do you think? We aren't allowed to leave the premises!

MILLIE (*indignantly*): Who says so?

HOWARD: Kershaw. He's just told me to spread it around.

MILLIE: And how does he think he's goin' to stop us?

HOWARD: Well, for a start, he's putting one of his men in the gate-lodge.

MILLIE: Flippin' cheek!

MISS TRANSOM: I can't hear a thing either of you's saying.

HOWARD (*loudly*): I was just telling Millie that Kershaw's stationed one of his men at the gate.

MISS TRANSOM: It's no use. I've lost my hearing-aid.

MILLIE (*loudly*): It's where you left it.

MISS TRANSOM (*cupping her ear*): Eh?

MILLIE (*bawling*): On the ledge in the downstairs Ladies'.

MISS TRANSOM: Oh yes, now I remember. (*Goes L. Stops and gives a witch-like chuckle*) All the same, I could get out of here any time I liked—without going through the gateway—or the tradesmen's door.

MILLIE: How?

MISS TRANSOM: Aha! That would be telling! (*With another gleeful chuckle she exits U.L.*)

MILLIE (*blankly*): What's she talkin' about? There *isn't* any other way out. (HOWARD *goes to french window and looks thoughtfully* OFF R. *for some moments. Then—*)

HOWARD: Of course! Of course!

MILLIE: Eh? (*Without heeding her* HOWARD *exits* OFF R., *not hurrying but clearly with a purpose in view.* ELSA *enters U.L.*)

ELSA: Have you seen Miss Harrington, Millie?

MILLIE: She's still in her room, I think. Here — do you think she *has* lost her memory?

ELSA: I don't know, Millie. I'm very worried about her.

MILLIE (*nods, sympathetically*): All right when you knew her at school, was she?

ELSA : Yes, full of energy, always happy, always ready to cheer you up if you weren't feeling well. A natural born nurse. That's why it's so upsetting to see her like this.

MILLIE : M'yes, funny thing, am— what's it?

ELSA : Amnesia.

MILLIE : I've heard they can forget who they are and where they come from—all their past lives.

ELSA : They're extreme cases. With Miss Harrington it can only be the result of the concussion.

MILLIE : So she might get her memory back any time?

ELSA : I'm sure she will. (*But she still looks very worried.* LAURA *enters R., carrying her handbag.* ELSA *watches her carefully*) See if coffee's on the way, Millie. (MILLIE *gives an understanding nod and exits U.L.* LAURA *puts her handbag on the table upstage and* ELSA *goes to her*) Try to relax, Laura.

LAURA : Relax!

ELSA : I know how you must be feeling, darling, but—

LAURA : Do you? Have you any idea what it's like to be caught up in a living nightmare? Everything that's happening to me is so unreal—so fantastic that I sometimes think I'm looking at a play on television—watching things happening to somebody else. But I'm not. It *is* real and it *is* happening to me. And—there just isn't anything I can do. (*She drops into a chair*)

ELSA : If you only had some relatives you could get in touch with. What about friends? Isn't there somebody you could get to come and stay with you for a few days while you rested?

LAURA : I've lost touch with my friends in this country while I've been living in Ireland. And I don't need rest.

ELSA : I think you do, darling.

LAURA (*tensely*): Elsa, Elsa — listen to me. I haven't lost my memory. Do you understand? I have not lost my memory— whatever Miss Prestwood may say.

ELSA : Well, she didn't actually say that. When you fainted and hit your head the concussion left you confused a little, but it'll only be temporary, and—

LAURA (*overlapping*): There was no concussion.

ELSA : But Laura—

LAURA (*overlapping, impatiently*): Oh, for Heaven's sake, Elsa! I'm a trained nurse!

ELSA : I know, And you kept saying you weren't, didn't you?

LAURA : Never mind about that now. Listen—with concussion there'd be other symptoms besides amnesia. Shock, slow reaction, poor co-ordination—several things. I've had no concussion, I tell you.

ELSA : Then what's the answer, Laura?

LAURA (*pacing away in agitation*): I don't know. I don't know! But everything I've told you is the truth—right from the time I met that woman in the cafe in Dublin.

ELSA : When you said you saw Annette Fielding?

LAURA : Yes. Why?

ELSA : Well, I didn't really want to tell you, but Annette's been able to prove that she was never anywhere near Dublin at that time. Since she came here with a spine injury, she's only once been away and that was to a specialist in London for a routine X-ray.

LAURA (uncertainly): Well, I could have been mistaken about her . . .

ELSA (nods): And don't you think that—

LAURA (overlapping): But not about the other things—and I tell you again, there's nothing wrong with my mind! That woman in the cafe—somebody sent her to tell me about Abbot's Mead, somebody who knew I needed a job pretty badly. The same person arranged for me to be drugged on the boat and a small fortune in diamonds planted in my case. Why — why? . . . Elsa — what do you know about this place?

ELSA : A doctor built it for mental cases. Then some years ago Miss Lorrimer took it over and ran it as a general nursing-home, registered with the County Health authorities. All above-board. I checked before I came. But it's all in those papers you brought with you.

LAURA : I didn't bring them with me. They were planted on me as well.

ELSA (gently): But, darling, when the Inspector showed you the lease and the transfer you identified the signatures on them as yours.

LAURA : I thought they were mine, at first. They looked exactly like mine. But they were forgeries. I've never seen any of those papers in my life before. (HOWARD enters by french window. LAURA paces away. Tensely—) What does it mean—what does it all mean?

ELSA (compassionately, putting an arm round LAURA): Try not to worry yourself too much, darling . . . I'll go and see about the coffee (She goes L. and sees HOWARD. Aside to him—) Don't leave her, Howard. (HOWARD nods. ELSA exits U.L.)

LAURA (with a bitter laugh): It's funny, isn't it?

HOWARD : What is?

LAURA : Everybody who's ever known me has always thought me so self-reliant. I thought I was, too. Capable, level-headed, calm in an emergency. That's what I was trained to be. But I'll never feel so sure of myself again. If there were just someone I could turn to so that I wouldn't feel so helpless.

HOWARD : If that's all that's worrying you, you haven't any problem.

LAURA (turns to him, hopefully): You mean you?

HOWARD : Me? Oh no. (LAURA's hopelessness fades) I shan't be around much longer.

LAURA : You mean you're leaving?

HOWARD : That's right.

LAURA : Why?

HOWARD : Just say that I've always made a point of not getting mixed up with stolen jewellery—especially when a Scotland Yard detective is interested.

LAURA (*bitterly*): I might have known you'd have been thinking of yourself.

HOWARD (*mildly surprised*): What's wrong with that?

LAURA : What did you mean by saying I had no problem?

HOWARD : Throw the ball back to Kershaw. Demand a full investigation into your Dublin background and prove that you're a law-abiding citizen with nothing to hide.

LAURA (*turning quickly away*): No.

HOWARD : But that's *bound* to help—

LAURA : No, I tell you! (HOWARD *looks at her back in silence, reflectively, for some moments. Then—*)

HOWARD : It's your party.

LAURA (*tensely*): There must be some way of proving my story. (*Racking her brain. Suddenly an idea strikes her*) Wait a minute! (MISS TRANSOM *appears in* ENTR. U.L. *Neither of the other two sees her*)

HOWARD : Got something?

LAURA : Yes . . . Yes, I think I have. The very first letter I had from Miss Prestwood. I've still got it.

HOWARD (*sharply*): I thought all the correspondence about that was in Kershaw's hands.

LAURA : All but this one. It was just a memo, in Miss Prestwood's handwriting, asking me to send in a formal application for the job of receptionist.

HOWARD : And you've still got it?

LAURA : Yes — I'm sure of it. It should be in my handbag. (*As she turns upstage* MISS TRANSOM *quickly withdraws* OFF L.) I put it in the wallet of my diary. (*She takes a pocket-diary out of her handbag*) Here it is. (*She comes back downstage, taking a folded slip of paper out of the wallet lining of the diary*) There you are —look! (*Without leaving go of the paper she holds it for* HOWARD *to see*)

HOWARD (*reading*): " Memo to Miss Laura Harrington. Re your enquiry about the vacancy for receptionist, if you will send in a formal application, giving details of your age, experience, etc., this will receive early attention."

LAURA : The signature! Look at the signature!

HOWARD : Margaret Prestwood . . . Well, that's quite interesting.

LAURA : Is that all you can say? Don't you see? This is proof, in black and white, that I applied for a job as receptionist and that Miss Prestwood knows very well I did! And that means proof that all those letters about me being the new owner of Abbot's Mead are all forgeries. (*She is folding the paper and putting it back in her diary*) Wait till I show Inspector Kershaw this!

KERSHAW (OFF L.) Where's Miss Harrington? (LAURA *goes upstage to her handbag and, without masking it, puts the diary inside*)

LAURA (going L.): Do you want me, Inspector? (*She exits U.L.* HOWARD *takes a few steps after her, looking thoughtful, then turns and, without haste, goes to the table on which* LAURA's *handbag lies. He looks down at it*)

KERSHAW (OFF L.): Yes, I'd like to talk to you, Miss Harrington (LAURA *reappears at* ENTR. U.L.)

LAURA (*looking back*): I'd rather like to talk to you as well, Inspector. (KERSHAW *enters U.L.*)

KERSHAW (*looking back*): I think you'd better come as well. (ELSA *enters, followed by* GRAHAM) And you, Miss Prestwood. (HOWARD *has been standing with his back to the audience, masking the handbag. He now moves away, without haste, but stays upstage.* MISS PRESTWOOD *enters U.L., following the others across the room.* KERSHAW *stays a few paces downstage from* ENTR. U.L.)

GRAHAM : Well, are you going to call it a day, old boy — er, Inspector? We've been pretty patient, but after all there is a limit. Personally, I'm beginning to feel like a ruddy ticket-of leave man or something.

KERSHAW : Sorry, sir, but I'm only doing my job.

ELSA (*crossing R.*): You're doing it pretty thoroughly too, aren't you? Detailed statements from everybody in the house about their background. I don't know how you haven't got writer's cramp.

KERSHAW : It's taken quite a bit of time but my orders were to check on everybody. (ELSA *sits at R.*)

LAURA : What do you mean by everybody?

KERSHAW (*mildly, slowly turning towards* LAURA): It's a clear and simply enough word, Miss Harrington?

LAURA : It means all the people staying here?

KERSHAW : Yes.

LAURA : And all the staff?

KERSHAW : Yes.

LAURA : Including . . . Miss Prestwood? (*Reaction from all the others except* HOWARD. LAURA *now feels sure of herself and speaks forcefully*)

KERSHAW (*still gently but shrewdly*): Why do you specially mention Miss Prestwood?

LAURA : I have a good reason.

MISS PRESTWOOD (*surprised and with prim firmness*): Really, Miss Harrington, I don't think I quite like your tone.

LAURA : Don't you?

GRAHAM : Inspector, can't we get on with it?

KERSHAW : Very well. Perhaps you'll be seated. (GRAHAM *sits on the arm of* ELSA's *chair.* LAURA *sits about C., and* MISS PRESTWOOD *at L.* HOWARD *stays upstage, standing*) Well, ladies and gentlemen, I dare say some of you have been wondering why a police officer from New Scotland Yard should come all the way out here. There are several reasons why he sometimes comes out of the Metropolitan Police District on an investigation, but two common ones are, first, when the Assistant Commissioner has been asked by another police authority to help in the investigation of a certain person and, second, where that person has entered the Metropolitan Police District, and has had to be traced from there.

LAURA : That rather points to me on both counts, doesn't it?

KERSHAW *(disregarding this)*: Yesterday morning we were alerted by the Dublin Police. They asked us for our help in connection with a matter which had been standing open in their books for some time—a big jewel robbery in County Clare.

GRAHAM ⎫ *(together)*: Good grief!
ELSA ⎭ A jewel robbery!

MISS PRESTWOOD : Then that's why you—

KERSHAW : The jewels were stolen from a country mansion. It was a family collection, quite famous in those parts and known as the Kerrigan Bounty, diamonds worthy sixty thousand pounds. *(Reaction from all but LAURA)* The Dublin police worked hard on the case but the jewels were never traced. It was believed they had been disposed of to a fence—a receiver called Jonas Donlevy—who was holding on to them until the heat had cooled off, so all the police there could do was to wait. Then, a short time ago, Donlevy died. The Dublin police kept a close watch on all his associates in case any of them should try to dispose of the Kerrigan diamonds but they drew a blank. Then only yesterday, they got a tip-off from an informer that an attempt was to be made to get the jewels out of Ireland and into England but he didn't know whether the carrier was to be a man, or . . . a woman. They kept a close watch on every possible suspect but without any result. Finally, they asked us to detain a woman at Fishguard. We moved as quickly as we could but it seems that because the woman had been taken ill on the boat—a fainting fit, it was—she was taken straight from the boat to a First Aid room and our men missed her. *(He pauses for some moments and then turns deliberately to LAURA)* Now, Miss Harrington, in view of all I've just said do you wish to reconsider any of the statements you've made to me?

LAURA : No. None.

MISS PRESTWOOD : But Miss Harrington, you—

KERSHAW *(overlapping)*: Please, Miss Prestwood, I'd like Miss Harrington to speak for herself. Now, Miss Harrington—think carefully.

LAURA : I told you I came here to take a job as a receptionist and it was true. *(She looks deliberately at MISS PRESTWOOD)* And Miss Prestwood knows perfectly well it's true. Don't, you Miss Prestwood?

MISS PRESTWOOD : No, I'm afraid I don't.

LAURA : And I can prove that you do!

MISS PRESTOOD *(regretfully)*: I'm afraid, Inspector — I don't like to say this — but I'm afraid Miss Harrington is trying to turn attention away from the jewellery, Inspector, and now you've

told us that that's the reason for your being here it's our duty
to tell you what we know about it.

HOWARD (*glancing round*): It seems you all know something. Miss
Milburn?

ELSA : Yes, we do. (*With a regretful look at* LAURA—) I'm sorry
Laura. (*To* KERSHAW—) Some jewellery—a lot—was found in
Miss Harrington's suitcase. (*Quickly, as* KERSHAW *turns to*
...LAURA—) But she knows nothing of how it got there.

GRAHAM : That's right, Inspector. It must have been planted in her
case when she was doped on the boat.

KERSHAW : Diamonds? (GRAHAM *nods*) Where are they now?

ELSA : Howard — Mr Carson — took charge of them.

KERSHAW (*turning in his unhurried way on* HOWARD): Oh? Why
did you do that, Mr Carson?

HOWARD : Somebody had to. That ancient safe in Miss Prestwood's
office can't be locked. The top drawer in my bedroom can.

KERSHAW : You didn't think of telling me about them?

HOWARD : Why should we? We didn't know then what you've
just told us now.

KERSHAW : True enough. Matter of fact, I didn't know the whole
picture myself until I telephoned my report up to London last
night. Well, in that case, Mr Carson, I must ask you for the
key to that drawer. (*He holds out his hand.* HOWARD *looks at
him, making no attempt to produce the key. Picture for some
moments, then* MILLIE *enters U.L.*)

MILLIE : There's a man here. Says his name's Stevens and he's
reportin' for orders.

KERSHAW : That'll be the other man the County Police have sent
me. Ask him to wait. (MILLIE *exits U.L.*) Mr. Carson? (HOWARD
takes a bunch of keys from his pocket and sorts them)

HOWARD : I'll go up and get the diamonds.

KERSHAW : The keys, Mr Carson. (HOWARD *is still for some moments then holds up the bunch by one of the keys*) Thank you.
Mr Peters, do you know the drawer Mr Carson means in his
room?

GRAHAM : What? Oh yes, I suppose so. (*To* HOWARD—) The top
one in the chest of drawers, old boy? (HOWARD *nods*)

KERSHAW : Perhaps you'll go up with Stevens. (*At* ENTR. U.L. *he
calls to* OFF) I want you to go upstairs with Mr Peters, Stevens.
He'll tell you all about it. (*He gives the keys to* GRAHAM, *who
exits U.L.*) I'm still just a little curious as to why you were so
anxious to keep those diamonds in your possession, Mr Carson.

HOWARD : There's no 'anxious' about it. I've told you—for safety.

KERSHAW : Had you any idea of their value?

HOWARD : I knew they hadn't been won at Bingo.

KERSHAW : H'm. All right, we'll leave it at that for the present.
(*He becomes his old genial self again*) Well, now that we've got
things sorted out perhaps we can all relax.

LAURA (*getting up*): You mean I can leave here?

ELSA : You don't want to leave, do you, Laura?

LAURA : I never wanted anything so much in my life.

KERSHAW (regretfully): I'm afraid I shall have to ask you to come with me to County Police Headquarters.

LAURA : I tell you I know nothing whatever about those diamonds.

KERSHAW : Well, perhaps we can deal with it later.

LAURA : We'll deal with it now!

KERSHAW (surprised at her forcefulness): Oh?

LAURA : I can prove that what I said about my coming here was true.

KERSHAW : How?

LAURA : By a letter sent to me by Miss Prestwood.

KERSHAW (taking the correspondence from his pocket): I've got all the letters here and I've been through them carefully.

LAURA : Those letters are faked—at least some of them are, the ones that try to make out I've taken over Abbot's Mead. But there's one letter that isn't among them. The very first one that was sent to me from this address! A memo in Miss Prestwood's handwriting — (MISS PRESTWOOD reacts)—telling me to send in a formal application for the vacancy of receptionist.

KERSHAW : And what have you got to say about that, Miss Prestwood?

MISS PRESTWOOD : I don't remember ever writing Miss Harrington to that effect.

LAURA : Don't you? Then perhaps your memory might be refreshed when I show you the letter.

KERSHAW : You have it?

LAURA : Yes, I have it. Right here. (She goes to the table, takes the diary from her handbag and takes the memo out of the wallet of the diary) There you are. (She holds the memo out to KERSHAW)

KERSHAW (taking the memo): Thank you. (He unfolds it and reads it)

LAURA : Well? Is that a memo from Miss Prestwood on the Abbot's Mead letter-heading?

KERSHAW : Yes, it is.

LAURA : Read what it says.

KERSHAW (reads): "Memo from Margaret Prestwood, Acting Matron." (LAURA gives a little nod) "Alterations in meal-times. Residents are asked to note that on and after Monday the twenty-first — "

LAURA (in horror): Oh, no — no — no!

KERSHAW : " — all meals will be served one half hour earlier than at present." (He looks sternly at LAURA, who is almost stupefied)

MISS PRESTWOOD (smoothly): I'm afraid, Inspector, that Miss Harrington is quite definitely suffering from the effects of concussion.

LAURA (nearly hysterical): You're lying! You're lying and you know it!

MISS PRESTWOOD : You'll have to make allowances, Inspector.

LAURA : Why are you doing this to me? You — you — (She rushes at Miss Prestwood)

Elsa (crying out and catching Laura as she passes in front of her): Laura! (Kershaw, too, catches Laura's shoulder)

Kershaw : Miss Harrington, this won't do, you know. I appreciate that you're confused but you'll really have to try to control yourself.

Elsa : Have you got to take her away, Inspector?

Kershaw : I'm afraid so. After all, the Kerrigan diamonds were found in her suitcase.

Elsa : I'm absolutely certain she knows nothing about how they got there.

Kershaw : Maybe. But it's still got to be investigated. (Not harshly, to Laura—) If you're ready, Miss Harrington . . .

Elsa : Wait! You must see she's in no state to be taken to a police station. Look — you've got the jewellery back — that must count for something, surely. Why can't you leave her here for a few days while you make your enquiries, or whatever you have to do? (Earnestly—) Inspector, she isn't well.

Kershaw (hesitantly): Well . . . perhaps on medical grounds. (Considers briefly, then nods) Very well.

~~Graham : Good show, Inspector~~

Kershaw : I'll leave Miss Harrington in your charge, Miss Prestwood, but of course I shall have to leave a couple of men on duty.

Miss Prestwood : I quite understand, Inspector.

Kershaw : That's it, then. (Not unkindly, to Laura, whose back is still turned) You understand the position, Miss Harrington? (Laura nods. Kershaw regains all his former geniality) Well, ladies and gentlemen, thank you all for your co-operation. I don't suppose I shall have to trouble you any more. (Graham enters U.L.)

Graham : They've gone !

Kershaw : What! (Reaction from the others)

Graham : The top drawer in Carson's room was open — pulled right out! It was empty — no sign of the diamonds! (All turn and look at Howard, who is upstage R. He is staring at Graham in genuine surprise and horror. Picture for a moment. Then Miss Transom appears at Entr. U.L. She moves slowly and not furtively. Nobody sees her. She stands watching, her face expressionless)

CURTAIN

END OF ACT TWO

ACT THREE

Scene 1. THE SAME NIGHT

(*Beyond the window, the curtains of which are open the garden scene is only just visible in the dark blue lighting. In the room one or two table-lamps are on and there is enough concealed lighting to show the figure of* MISS TRANSOM. *She wears her hearing-aid and she is standing with her left side to the audience watching through the open french window to* OFF R., *very intently.* ANNETTE *enters* U.L., *walking slowly, pre-occupied. She is almost* C., *when she becomes aware of* MISS TRANSOM. *She watches her curiously for some moments*)

ANNETTE : What are you looking at?

MISS TRANSOM (*startled*): Oh! I didn't hear you come in.

ANNETTE : Is there somebody out there?

MISS TRANSOM (*hastily*): Oh, no, no, no. I — I was just thinking what a nice, quiet night it was. (ANNETTE *clearly doesn't believe her. She goes to french window and looks through to* OFF R.) (*Slyly*—) What you really want to know is whether Mr Peters is taking a stroll in the garden and, if so, whether anybody is with him.

ANNETTE (*angrily, turning away*): I don't know what you're talking about.

MISS TRANSOM (*chuckling*): I may be a little hard of hearing, but my eyes don't miss much, and they tell me that a certain young lady is jealous of a certain other young lady. (*Goes back to look through the french window*)

ANNETTE : It's a pity they don't tell you to mind your own business.

MISS TRANSOM (*watching* OFF R.): What did you say, dear?

ANNETTE : Oh, never mind.

MISS TRANSOM : Such an exciting day it's been, hasn't it? Scotland Yard detectives, signed statements, plain-clothes men searching all our rooms for diamonds—why, if we'd only had a few advertisements for washing-powders, it would have been as good as a thriller on television. But I was disappointed when Inspector Kershaw didn't take my dabs.

ANNETTE : Your what?

MISS TRANSOM : My dabs. Criminal jargon for fingerprints, dear. (GRAHAM *appears in* ENTR. U.L. *His pipe is in his mouth and he gets out his pouch*) Fancy me knowing more than a clever young woman like you. But then, perhaps there are some things I know that other people don't. Yes, indeed. (GRAHAM *strolls in and she sees him*) Ah! Enter Mr Peters, exit Thelma Transom! (*Going* R.)

GRAHAM : Why?

MISS TRANSOM : Because two's company and three's a crowd! (*With her witch-like chuckle she exits R.)*

GRAHAM *(watching after her)*: What was all that about knowing something?

ANNETTE *(going to* GRAHAM*)*: Graham, I want to talk to you.

GRAHAM : Well? *(Busy with his pipe)*

ANNETTE : We can't go on like this. At least, I can't. I've watched you and Elsa together—seen the way you look at her when she gives you one of those special smiles of hers. It's building up to something, isn't it, Graham?

GRAHAM : I wouldn't say that, exactly.

ANNETTE : Oh, don't keep putting me off—please. Tell me the truth.

GRAHAM : Frankly, old girl, it doesn't do much good telling you anything. You know me—I'm the friendly type. I like Elsa, and —well, there it is. I mean—

ANNETTE : Do you love her, that's what I want to know?

GRAHAM : Well, I wouldn't go so far as to say that—

ANNETTE *(hopefully, going nearer to him)*: Then there's still a chance? For you and me, I mean?

GRAHAM : Now look, Annette—don't let's get too serious about things, shall we—

ANNETTE : Don't you think I've the right to be serious?

GRAHAM : Well, I think we've got to keep a sense of proportion.

ANNETTE *(losing patience)*: Will you give me a straight answer? Is it over? *(*GRAHAM *does not answer.* ANNETTE *falls back a step as she reads the answer in* GRAHAM'S *silence.* ELSA *enters quickly U.L.)*

ELSA : Graham, have you— *(She stops abruptly as she takes in the situation.* ANNETTE, *disregarding her, keeps looking at* GRAHAM *for some moments, hoping against hope, then turns and exits R.)* Is Annette being difficult?

GRAHAM : Yes, she is a bit.

ELSA : I was afraid of this, you know, Graham.

GRAHAM : I wouldn't worry. She'll get over it. Did you want me?

ELSA : Yes. Will you move your car so that I can get mine into the garage? I don't want to leave it out there all night—it looks as though it could rain.

GRAHAM : Will do. *(Kisses her briefly on the cheek and exits U.L., followed by* ELSA*)*

ELSA *(as she goes out)*: I'd have moved it myself only you hadn't left the key in. *(The stage is empty for some moments, then a dark figure appears beyond french window. He looks back to* OFF R. *as though watching to see whether he has been followed, then enters. It is* HOWARD *dressed in dark trousers and a black jersey, with a dark neck-silk. His hair is dishevelled and there is a long smear of dust on his trouser-leg. He is panting with his exertions and has clearly been running a long way. He goes to a table or chair and supports himself by it as he recovers his breath.* MISS TRANSOM *enters R. She watches* HOWARD, *who has his back half-turned away and does not see her. Presently he*

recovers and smoothes back his hair. He is almost composed.
when—)

MISS TRANSOM *(searching in her workbag)*: Would you like me to lend you a comb, Mr Carson?

HOWARD *(turning quickly)*: What? Oh . . . No, it's all right, thanks.

MISS TRANSOM : I haven't seen you all evening. I was beginning to get quite worried about you.

HOWARD : I — er — I had rather a nasty headache. I thought I'd go and lie down in my room. Then I must have dropped off to sleep.

MISS TRANSOM : But your bedroom door was locked. I tried it.

HOWARD : I — yes, I locked the door so that I shouldn't be disturbed.

MISS TRANSOM *(beaming)*: And you weren't disturbed, were you, Mr Carson? You couldn't have been, because you weren't in your room.

HOWARD : Oh, wasn't I?

MISS TRANSOM *(slyly)*: No, you weren't Mr Carson—because I unlocked your door and peeped inside.

HOWARD : You unlocked my door?

MISS TRANSOM : Oh yes.

HOWARD : You mean you have a key that fits? (MISS TRANSOM *brings a bunch of keys out of her handbag)*

MISS TRANSOM : I have a lot of keys that will fit a lot of doors, Mr Carson. I've been here a long time, you know, and collecting keys is a hobby of mine. *(There is a brief silence while HOWARD watches MISS TRANSOM, without his expression giving anything away)*

MISS TRANSOM *(chuckling gleefully)*: You've been out in the grounds, trying to get away, haven't you, Mr Carson?

HOWARD : Now what gave you that idea?

MISS TRANSOM : Haven't you, Mr Carson?

HOWARD : This place was built for mental patients — remember? Ten foot wall, barbed wire on top.

MISS TRANSOM *(tauntingly)*: But there are other ways out.

HOWARD *(nods)*: The tradesman's door in the front wall, and Kershaw's had that padlocked. That only leaves the main entrance.

MISS TRANSOM : Does it, Mr Carson?

HOWARD : And he's got his two men there in the lodge. And anyway—why should I want to get away?

MISS TRANSOM : Ah! Why indeed? (HOWARD *studies her, still without his own expression giving anything away)* Tell me, Mr Carson—those diamonds that disappeared from your bedroom. Have you any idea where they are?

HOWARD : Why should I have?

MISS TRANSOM : Aha! And again I say—why indeed? (MILLIE *enters U.L.)*

MILLIE *(bitterly)*: Well, if ever I'm workin' in a place again where they're goin' to have a police search I shall ask for me cards before they even start! Talk about turnin' the place upside down!

HOWARD : Well, if you'll excuse me, Miss Transom, I've got to see Miss Prestwood. (*Going R.*)

MISS TRANSOM : Oh? Something important.

HOWARD : You might call it that.

MISS TRANSOM : Oh. Well, don't forget to brush the mud off your trouser-leg, will you? (HOWARD *glances down, brushes the mud with his hand, looks back at* MISS TRANSOM *and exits R.* MILLIE *is watching* MISS TRANSOM'S *sly look*)

MILLIE (*suspiciously*): Here—what are you up to?

MISS TRANSOM : Up to?

MILLIE : Come on—come on, I know that artful look of yours!

MISS TRANSOM (*conspiratorially*): Shall I tell you something, Millie?

MILLIE : What?

MISS TRANSOM : There are those among us who are not what they pretend to be. (*She tiptoes R., stops and puts her finger over her lips*) Sssh! (*She tiptoes out R.*)

MILLIE : I wonder what it feels like to be halfway round the twist. (*Shaking her head she remembers why she came and turns L. again*) Here—do you want hot milk last thing or cocoa? (*But* MISS TRANSOM *has gone*) Okay, you'll get cocoa and like it. (LAURA *enters U.L.*) Hallo, Miss Harrington, Did you find your room okay? I tidied up for you after them coppers had finished.

LAURA : Yes. Thank you, Millie.

MILLIE : Talk about goin' through the place with a fine-tooth comb! Carpets up, loose cushions out—they even had some of the floor-boards up. Here, Miss Harrington—where d'you reckon that jewellery went to?

LAURA (*wearily*): I've no idea, Millie.

MILLIE (*sympathetically*): Sorry, Miss Harrington, I shouldn't have mentioned it. Is there anythin' you'd like me to get you?

LAURA : No, nothing.

MILLIE : Well, I'll be gettin' along then. (*Goes L.*) Have a couple of aspirins and go to bed early. I'm sure it'll do you good. (*She lets* ELSA *enter U.L., then exits U.L.*)

ELSA : Well, it took me a lot longer to straighten my room out than it took those detectives to wreck it. They searched in places I never even dreamed existed. (*She goes towards the french window*) I wonder how they train them.

LAURA : Elsa.

ELSA (*stopping*): Yes?

LAURA : Are you going out?

ELSA : We can't go out—had you forgotten? Kershaw's got men stationed out there to see that we don't. I was just going to put my car away.

LAURA : Stay and talk to me, Elsa.

ELSA : Of course. (*She comes and sits near where* LAURA *is standing. Sympathetically—*) What is it, darling?

LAURA : I— (*With a worried little laugh*) —well, I just wanted to talk. I — I felt so alone, and — well, I know we haven't seen each other for years, but—

ELSA : We were friends at school.

LAURA : Yes . . . Oh Elsa, I'm so frightened.

ELSA : Try not to worry too much, darling. Those diamonds are here somewhere. Kershaw and his men are bound to find them tomorrow, then they'll go away.

LAURA : That's only part of it. *(She paces away)* I want to know what's happening to me. Why am I here? What horrible thing's going to happen next? Have you any idea what I feel like— knowing that somebody has come into my life, somebody who knows all about me, but I don't know them. They've got everything worked out—everything planned and organized so efficiently that they can use me for their purpose—and I can't even guess what that purpose is. I feel like—like a puppet being made to move about—dance, run, walk—and I don't know who's working the strings. *(She has worked herself up to a high pitch of tension.* ELSA *reaches up and clasps her hand comfortingly)*

ELSA : I know it's dreadful for you, darling, but I'm sure everything will straighten itself out quite soon.

LAURA : I'm going to get out of here, Elsa.

ELSA *(gently)*: But you can't, dear.

LAURA : I'll find a way. I don't know how, but I will. *(Pacing agitatedly upstage she stops suddenly as she looks through french window to* OFF R.) Is that your car out there?

ELSA : Yes.

LAURA : Is the key in it?

ELSA : Yes, it is. But why—

LAURA *(overlapping)*: Can I take it? Only to get to the railway station. You could pick it up there.

ELSA : But they wouldn't let you out of the grounds—

LAURA : How could they stop me? I could rush the front entrance— *(*ELSA *goes to her)* the gates are always open—

ELSA *(gently)*: Come and sit down. *(*LAURA *allows herself to be led downstage and sits)* Now, you sit quietly while I go and get Miss Prestwood to give you something. *(Goes* L.)

LAURA : No! *(*ELSA *stops)* I don't want to be left alone. Come back, Elsa. *(*ELSA *slowly returns* C.) It's all right—I'm not going to get hysterical. I told you—I just want to talk to somebody. Yes, that's it. Let me talk—let me go through the whole thing, right from the beginning.

ELSA : Yes, that might help. *(She sits)*

LAURA : There must be some sort of a pattern—a plan. It started with that middle-aged woman who came and sat at my table in the O'Connell Street cafe. She was sent by—whoever's behind all this, to contact me.

ELSA : Why do you think that?

LAURA : She asked me if I knew anything about nursing.

ELSA : And you said you did?

LAURA : No. That's the whole point. I said I didn't.

ELSA : But you're a State Registered Nurse.

LAURA : Yes, but . . . well, I didn't want that to be known.

ELSA : Why ever not?

LAURA : I had a reason. But that's why I'm so sure she was part of this whole-set-up. She *knew* I was a nurse, else why would she start up a conversation with me—a total stranger—by asking if I knew anything about nursing? If I'd admitted that I did, she'd have said they wanted a qualified nurse at Abbot's Mead. When I said I'd been working as a secretary, she said there was a job going here as a receptionist—much the same thing. Don't you see? Then I got in touch with Miss Prestwood and, after several letters passed between us I got the job. Then comes the second stage of the operation.

ELSA : And what was that?

LAURA : Miss Prestwood was very insistent that I should bring all the correspondence with me—in fact she made it a condition of my employment.

ELSA : The correspondence was to identify you. Nothing strange about that, surely.

LAURA : That's what I thought at the time. But I could have proved my identity by my passport—my driving-licence—lots of things. But now, after all that's happened, I realize that making sure I brought the correspondence was important.

ELSA : Why?

LAURA : So that it could be taken out of my case on my way here and I'd be left without a shred of evidence that I'd come to take up a routine job as receptionist.

ELSA (*nods*): Yes, I see that.

LAURA : Next, I was drugged on the boat coming over, very likely by someone dressed as a stewardess. Then she takes off her uniform, mixes with the passengers who took me to the First Aid Room at Fishguard and, while they were trying to bring me round, she puts the Kerrigan diamonds in my suitcase and sub-stitutes the fake letters for the genuine ones. That wouldn't take long, would it?

ELSA : No. Only a few minutes, if that's what *did* happen.

LAURA (*pacing upstage, striving to think*): It makes sense about the diamonds. They were using me as the carrier. But those papers! Why are they so anxious to prove that I'm a qualified nurse and that I've taken over Abbot's Mead Convalescent Home?

ELSA : But your signature on the transfer.

LAURA : I've told you—it wasn't mine. It wasn't.

ELSA : Then what about that—what was his name? Mr Wether-burn, who interviewed you in Dublin?

LAURA : Nobody interviewed me in Dublin.

ELSA : But Miss Prestwood said—

LAURA : Yes! Miss Prestwood said. It always comes back to what Miss Prestwood said—have you noticed? (*She sees* ELSA *giving her a doubtful look*) What's the matter? Why are you looking at me like that? Oh yes, it's that concussion that's still bothering you, isn't it? Another of the things that Miss Prestwood talked about. Well, I've been thinking about that.

ELSA : Well, after all, nobody could arrange *that*.

LAURA : Nobody did. Listen—after I'd been drugged on board, I fell and banged my head. Several of the other passengers saw me, and so did the woman who put the stuff in my coffee. Suppose she telephoned to Miss Prestwood to tell her? That would be a *real* bonus for her, wouldn't it?

ELSA : What do you mean by a bonus?

LAURA: It was far too good a chance for her to miss. She improvised —spread it around to you, and later to Kershaw, that the blow on the head had caused loss of memory. Who would believe anything I said after that?

ELSA : It's — it's all so . . .

LAURA : So what?

ELSA : I — I don't know what to think. I want to believe you, of course, Laura, but—

LAURA : All these things haven't convinced you, have they? Well, here's something that concerns *you*.

ELSA : Me?

LAURA : You said that you'd written to me in Dublin.

ELSA : That's right. Miss Prestwood happened to mention that she was in touch with a Laura Harrington, a State Registered nurse. Yours isn't a common name and I knew you'd gone in for nursing, so I was pretty sure it was you. But I wrote to you to make sure.

LAURA : And I told you—I never got that letter. Now: did you post it yourself?

ELSA : No. You see, we always put our letters in the mail-tray in the hall and Miss Prestwood sends them in to the village Post Office.

LAURA : So it would be simple for her to make sure that your letter never got posted at all?

ELSA : But why would she do that?

LAURA : She'd told you I was coming here as a qualified nurse, to take over Abbot's Mead. You were bound to say something about that when you wrote to me and I'd have known there was something odd going on.

ELSA : But you wrote to me in reply.

LAURA : Did I? Have you still got my letter?

ELSA : No. No, I haven't. Actually, it wasn't a separate letter to me, at all. Miss Prestwood said you'd written a note for me on the back of one of your letters to her. She gave it to me to read but, of course, she kept it. (*She stops abruptly*) You mean—

LAURA (*nods*): A fake, like all the other letters. Now are you convinced.

ELSA : It's almost unbelievable! But you must be right. But why, Laura — why? And think of all the planning and organization it would take.

LAURA : Sixty thousand pounds in diamonds is worth a lot of

planning. And she wasn't in it alone.

ELSA : You mean there's someone else?

LAURA : Elsa . . . what do you know about Howard Carson?

ELSA : Laura!

LAURA : How much do you know about him?

ELSA : I — well, very little, I suppose, really. He's with a London firm of underwriters, I think. He'd been over-working and he had a nervous breakdown. Why do you ask about Howard Carson?

LAURA : I had proof, certain proof, that my story about coming here as a receptionist was true—a memo on Abbot's Mead letter-heading, written by Miss Prestwood herself. When I took it out of my diary and gave it to Inspector Kershaw it turned out to be only a notice about the change of meal-times.

ELSA : Yes, I remember. What has that to do with Howard?

LAURA : He was the only one who knew anything about that memo. I showed it to him. He saw me put it in my handbag. He was the only one who went anywhere near it.

ELSA : You think he and Miss Prestwood are connected?

LAURA : Think? (*She goes upstage*) I'm at the stage when I'm terrified to think. (ELSA *goes quickly to her*)

ELSA : Laura—

LAURA : I must get away from here I tell you!

ELSA : Laura, listen to me! . . . I believe what you've told me.

LAURA (*turning, calming down*): You do?

ELSA : Yes. You've convinced me.

LAURA : Well, that's something. It makes me feel not quite so alone.

ELSA : You're not alone, darling. Now, I'll tell you what I'm going to do. You may think Graham's an easy-going casual type but he can be very capable when he wants to. I'm going to tell him the whole story and get him to help. But I want you to promise me something.

LAURA : What is it?

ELSA : Not to do anything impulsive, like trying to get away on your own, until I've seen Graham.

LAURA : All right. (ELSA *smiles and gives* LAURA *a comforting hug*)

ELSA : I won't be long. (*She exits U.L.* LAURA *goes to french window and gazes out at* ELSA's *car once again. For some moments she struggles with herself in indecision then is seen to make her resolve. She turns and goes quickly L. As she gets to* ENTR. *U.L. she suddenly stops with a gasp as she sees who is beyond. Still staring through to* OFF L., *she falls back a step, then another. Then* MISS PRESTWOOD *slowly enters. For the first time* MISS PRESTWOOD *seems a faintly sinister figure. She is no longer fussy and prim and her voice has a hard edge to it*)

MISS PRESTWOOD : Going somewhere, Miss Harrington?

LAURA : No . . . no.

MISS PRESTWOOD : I must have been mistaken. You seemed to be in a hurry.

LAURA : I — I must go to my room. (*Forcing herself to walk at*

normal pace she passes Miss Prestwood *and exits* U.L. Miss
Prestwood *stands motionless. In some strange way she seems
suddenly to have become a dominating personality.* Miss
Transom *enters* R., *carrying a workbag)*

Miss Transom : Ah, there you are, Miss Prestwood.

Miss Prestwood : Millie said you wished to see me.

Miss Transom : Indeed, indeed I did, Miss Prestwood. *(With
elaborate stealth she creeps to* Entr. U.L. *and looks* Off *to
make sure no-one is about)*

Miss Prestwood : What is all that for?

Miss Transom : You can't be too careful.

Miss Prestwood : Why should you be careful?

Miss Transom *(tiptoeing back* C.): Because I don't want anybody
esle to know that I've got— *(Mysteriously, with a furtive glance
round, as she puts her hand into her workbag)*— you-know-what!

Miss Prestwood *(sternly)*: Miss Transom, will you please tell me
what you're talking about?

Miss Transom : With pleasure, Miss Prestwood. *(She brings out
her hand, holding the jewellery)* This!

Miss Prestwood : The Kerrigan diamonds!

Miss Transom *(slyly, nodding)*: The Kerrigan diamonds.

Miss Prestwood : Where did you get them?

Miss Transom : From Mr Carson's room.

Miss Prestwood : You mean it was you who broke into his chest
of drawers?

Miss Transom : I didn't break into it. I unlocked it. You'd be surprised at the number of different keys I've got.

Miss Prestwood : But Inspector Kershaw's men ransacked he
place for those diamonds. Your room was searched, like everybody else's.

Miss Transom : Yes, I know. But before they came to my
room, I went and put the jewellery in somebody else's room
that they'd already searched.

Miss Prestwood : Whose ?

Miss Transom : Yours.

Miss Prestwood : What !

Miss Transom : Wasn't that cunning of me ?

Miss Prestwood : Where did you hide it ?

Miss Transom : Inside that green hat on your wardrobe shelf. I
never did like you in that hat, Miss Prestwood. Green makes
you look bilious.

Miss Prestwood *(controlling herself with difficulty)*: I suppose
there's not much point in asking how you got into my room ?

Miss Transom : None whatever. I *said* you'd be surprised how
many keys I'd got, didn't I ? *(She gives the jewellery to* Miss
Prestwood) : There you are.

Miss Prestwood : Why did you take these from Mr Carson's
room ?

Miss Transom : Because I was so sorry for poor Miss Harrington,
you see ?

MISS PRESTWOOD : No, I certainly do *not* see.

MISS TRANSOM : Well, she seemed in such terrible trouble. I thought if the diamonds condn't be found, Inspector Kershaw wouldn't be able to charge her with anything. No diamonds, no evidence. You see ? Then I thought it over and I decided I'd better turn the whole thing over to you.

MISS PRESTWOOD : I see. Very wise of you, Miss Transom.

MISS TRANSOM : I'm so glad you think so, Miss Prestwood *(She beams happily)* What are you going to do with the jewellery ? *(MISS PRESTWOOD is thinking deeply and does not reply)* Are you going to ring up Inspector Kershaw at the Black Bull ?

MISS PRESTWOOD : No.

MISS TRANSOM : Why not ?

MISS PRESTWOOD : It can wait till morning.

MISS TRANSOM *(shyly)* : No good putting it in the safe in your office. It doesn't lock.

MISS PRESTWOOD : I shall put it in the steel medicine cabinet. Nobody has a key to that but me. *(She looks sternly at* MISS TRANSOM) Now listen to me, Miss Transom.

MISS TRANSOM : Yes ?

MISS PRESTWOOD : You're to tell nobody about this, do you understand ? Nobody.

MISS TRANSOM : I shan't breathe a word.

MISS PRESTWOOD : See that you don't. Otherwise you'll be very sorry, believe me. If I tell Inspector Kershaw that you took the diamonds from Mr Carson's room, you'll be charged with being an accessory.

MISS TRANSOM *(looking scared)* : Oh !

MISS PRESTWOOD *(warningly)* : So remember ! *(MISS TRANSOM nods. MISS PRESTWOOD exits U.L.)*

MISS TRANSOM : Accessory ? *(She goes to* ENTR. *U.L. and watches. OFF.* HOWARD *enters R.)*

HOWARD : Hallo, what are you up to ?

MISS TRANSOM : Beg pardon, Mr Carson ?

HOWARD : Come on, come on—turn up your hearing-aid. I asked you what you were up to ? I know that leery look of yours.

MISS TRANSOM *(with wide-eyed innocence)* : I was talking to Miss Prestwood, that's all.

HOWARD : Oh, I've been looking for her all over the place. *(Goes L.)*

MISS TRANSOM : What do you want her for, Mr Carson ?

HOWARD : To tell her I'm leaving tomorrow.

MISS TRANSOM : If Inspector Kershaw lets you.

HOWARD : We can but try. *(Turns L. again to go out)*

MISS TRANSOM : I took the diamonds out of your room, Mr Carson. *(HOWARD stops dead but does not turn. He does not speak for quite a while. Then —)*

HOWARD : What did you do with them ?

MISS TRANSOM *(mockingly)* : At one time I used to have your room, you know. I've got all the keys.

HOWARD (*tonelessly, still not turning*): I said, what did you do with the diamonds?

MISS TRANSOM : I gave them to Miss Prestwood. (HOWARD *stands motionless, still turning towards L. The silence causes MISS TRANSOM to lose a little of her confidence. At last HOWARD turns and walks slowly towards MISS TRANSOM. She cowers just a little but stands her ground. Deliberately, and without haste HOWARD raises his arms and puts his two hands round MISS TRANSOM's throat. He speaks without passion but with deadly seriousness*)

HOWARD : You know, Miss Transom . . . I ought to kill you. (MISS TRANSOM's *eyes open wide as* HOWARD *holds her by the throat, though he exerts no pressure. At last he lowers his arms and, without hurrying, exits U.L. MISS TRANSOM slowly relaxes—very slowly indeed—and lets out a very audible sigh of relief. She swallows hard, trips over to* ENTR. *U.L. and peers off after* HOWARD, *then comes back C. she thinks things over for a while, then her sly look returns and she chuckles to herself. She goes R. and exits by* DOOR R., *still chuckling. The room is empty for a short while then* LAURA *enters U.L. She wears her coat and carries her handbag which she sets down on a table while she fastens her coat. She looks through window to* OFF R. *to make sure that* ELSA's *car is still there. Having fastened her coat she comes back, gets her handbag, then with a last look to off L. she goes quickly out by french window and exits* OFF R.)

ELSA (OFF L.): Laura. (*Nearer*—) Laura. (*She enters and looks round.* GRAHAM *enters, followed by* MILLIE) She isn't here.

GRAHAM : Are you sure you saw Miss Harrington come in here, Millie?

MILLIE : 'Course I'm sure. Looked in a right state she did.

GRAHAM : What do you mean by that?

MILLIE : All sort of keyed up—you know what I mean? Very pale, she was. (MISS TRANSOM *enters R.*)

MISS TRANSOM : What is Miss Fielding doing in your car?

ELSA : Annette? Are you sure?

MISS TRANSOM : Well, I saw her out on the drive.

ELSA : Laura! Graham—it isn't Annette in my car! It's Laura! (GRAHAM *hurries to french window, followed by* ELSA. *He looks through to* OFF R. *If desired there may be the sound of a car engine revving up*)

GRAHAM : She's driving off! (*Calls*—) Laura! Look out! (*He runs out* OFF R., *calling*—) Laura! (MILLIE *and* MISS TRANSOM *have gone to the window. They ad lib in character. Suddenly there is a scream from* ANNETTE OFF R.)

MILLIE : That's Miss Fielding!

ELSA : Annette! (*She hurries out by french window.* MISS PRESTWOOD *enters U.L.*)

MISS PRESTWOOD : What's the matter—what's going on? (*She is composed but watchful*)

MILLIE : It's Miss Harrington. She drove off in Miss Milburn's car, and — and —

MISS PRESTWOOD : Who was that who screamed?

MISS TRANSOM: It was Miss Fielding. I think the car must have hit her.

MISS PRESTWOOD : Oh no! (*She goes to french window and looks* OFF. MILLIE *and* MISS TRANSOM *do the same. All wait anxiously. Then* LAURA, *without her handbag, enters, followed by* ELSA. *The others separate to allow them an unmasked entrance.* ELSA'S *arm is round* LAURA, *who is dazed*)

LAURA : I never saw her—I never saw her at all —

ELSA : Miss Prestwood! (MISS PRESTWOOD *comes to* LAURA)

MISS PRESTWOOD : Come and sit down, Miss Harrington.

LAURA (*dazedly*): I don't know where she came from. I never felt the car hit her— (MISS PRESTWOOD *puts her in a chair*)

MISS PRESTWOOD : Don't talk about it now. (GRAHAM, *unmasked, enters. He carries* ANNETTE, *whose head is hanging back lifelessly. He pauses upstage for some moments then comes downstage.* ELSA *feels* ANNETTE'S *pulse with one hand; with the other she raises one of* ANNETTE'S *eyelids. There is a silence. Then—*)

ELSA : She's dead.

(LAURA *gives a choked sob and a shuddering —* " No — no — no!")

CURTAIN

END OF ACT THREE. SCENE I.

ACT THREE

(The stage is empty for some moments. Then—)

Miss Transom (Off L.): Millie . . . Millie. *(She enters U.L. and starts searching on tables and elsewhere. Millie enters U.L.)*
Millie : What do you want then?
Miss Transom : I've lost my hearing-aid.
Millie : What, again?
Miss Transom : I must find it. It's the only one I've got left that works. *(Searching all over)*
Millie : Have they heard— *(More loudly—)* Have they heard anythin' more from the hospital about Miss Fielding?
Miss Transom : I don't think so.
Millie : Coo, my stomach turned right over last night when they thought she was dead. Bit o' luck for her we'd got our own private ambulance here, wasn't it?
Miss Transom : No, no, not luck. Nursing-homes often have their own ambulances. I was in ours once—when I had a growling appendix. *(She suddenly stops searching and looks up, struck with a sudden thought)* Nursing home . . . Nursing home!
Millie : Heard about Miss Prestwood findin' them diamonds, did you?
Miss Transom : Eh?
Millie *(loudly)* : I said did you hear about Miss Prestwood finding them sparklers?
Miss Transom *(with overdone astonishment)* : No? Really? Where?
Millie : I dunno. Must 'a been some place them coppers missed. She telephoned Kershaw at the " Black Bull " and he's coming to get 'em. Here—that reminds me. We'll be able to get out of here now, won't we? Bloomin' good job, too. It was beginning to feel like being in a concentration camp. *(The telephone-bell rings)* Hallo—that'll be the hospital. *(Going to the 'phone)*
Miss Transom : I've remembered where I've left my hearing-aid. On the table in the hall. *(She exits R.)*
Millie *(into 'phone)*: Abbot's Mead Convalescent Home. How is she? . . . Miss Fielding, o' course. Aren't you the hospital then? Oh. Well, hang on a minute. *(Miss Prestwood enters U.L.)*
Miss Prestwood : Was that the telephone, Millie?
Millie : Yes, it's for you, Miss Prestwood. The County Health Department. *(Gives her the telephone)*
Miss Prestwood : Oh. Yes. *(Millie exits U.L. while she speaks)* Hallo, is that the County Health Department? Miss

Prestwood speaking. (*She is using her prim, polite style*) Did you get my letter? . . . Oh, you did. Yes, the new proprietor is Miss Laura Harrington, as I told you. If you look up her name in the . . . You've what? Oh, I see — you've been in touch with the hospital where she did her training, is that it? Then you'll know all about her . . . Yes, indeed . . . Yes, she is young, but very capable . . . Yes, the lease has been transferred to her. We'll send you a copy for your files and Miss Harrington will sign it . . . Not at all, not at all, that's quite all right. I realize your department has to be satisfied about these things. I'm only sorry we had to keep you waiting so long. (LAURA *enters U.L.*) Yes. Thank you, Goodbye. (*She sees* LAURA *and her manner hardens*)

LAURA (*anxiously*): How is she? (MISS PRESTWOOD *is puzzled*) Wasn't that the hospital?

MISS PRESTWOOD: Oh—yes. Yes, the hospital, of course. Miss Fielding is about the same.

LAURA: Is she still unconcious?

MISS PRESTWOOD: Yes.

LAURA: When will they know anything?

MISS PRESTWOOD: Impossible to say, with a skull fracture of that type. (LAURA *nods. She is desperately worried*) You ought ʰo know that. Or do you still persist in denying that you're a trained nurse?

LAURA: How it happened I just don't know. I never saw her—I didn't even know I'd hit her until I heard her scream. But I suppose I was—

MISS PRESTWOOD: You were at a high pitch of nervous tension. Was that what you were going to say, Miss Harrington?

LAURA (*with a sudden impassioned outburst*): With good reason, and you ought to know!

MISS PRESTWOOD: And you ought to have known better than to drive a car in that state. Trying to storm your way out like that, after Inspector Kershaw had forbidden you to leave (*Going L.*) Well, there's no question of your leaving after this (*She is about to exit U.L., when* HOWARD *enters, carrying a filled hold-all or suitcase.* MISS PRESTWOOD *immediately puts on her polite manner*) Ah, Mr Carson.

HOWARD: Did you 'phone Inspector Kershaw, Miss Prestwood?

MISS PRESTWOOD: Yes. It's perfectly in order for you to leave whenever you wish, Mr Carson.

HOWARD: Good. Thanks for your help.

MISS PRESTWOOD: Are you sure you won't stay for lunch?

HOWARD: I don't think so. I've loaded all my other stuff into the car—all ready for off, so there's no point in hanging about.

MISS PRESTWOOD: Then I'll say goodbye. It's been a pleasure to have you with us, Mr Carson and I'm glad you've made such good progress.

HOWARD: Thanks to you, Miss Prestwood. (MISS PRESTWOOD *beams, highly gratified*) If any of my friends want to get away from it all, I'll recommend them to Abbot's Mead.

MISS PRESTWOOD : Goodbye, Mr Carson. A pleasant journey. (*She exits U.L.* HOWARD *goes R., glancing at* LAURA, *then sets his case down. He watches* LAURA *in silence for some moments*)

HOWARD : You look just about flaked out, you know. (LAURA *does not answer, or look at him. He goes to her chair*) Is there any news of Annette?

LAURA : There's no change.

HOWARD : Well, I suppose it could be worse . . Look, I know you've had a pretty rough time since you came. I wish I could have helped you in some way. Before I go, I'd like you to know that I hope everything works out all right. (LAURA *still does not reply.* HOWARD *makes as though to speak again, then gives it up*) Well . . . .goodbye. (*He turns aside for his case*)

LAURA : Do you have to go?

HOWARD : I'm quite fit again. Anyway, near enough. And my firm want me back. (*He goes near her again*) Why did you ask that?

LAURA : Never mind. It doesn't matter.

HOWARD : I know it sounds silly, but — well, it sounded as though you didn't *want* me to go.

LAURA : I just suddenly felt . . . so alone, when I realized you were going. (*She forces a laugh*) That sounds silly too, doesn't it?

HOWARD : Well, it surprises me a bit, anyhow.

LAURA : You know, I didn't like you very much, at first. At least I *thought* I didn't. You sounded cynical—insincere, even selfish. Then — oh, I don't know, but I got the idea that it was all an act — that you weren't like that at all, really. I was . . . (*She breaks off*)

HOWARD : Yes?

LAURA : Well, I was going to ask you to be on my side. Just that. I don't know what you could have done, because I don't know what anyone could have done. But I just wanted someone to talk to. (*She is not looking at* HOWARD. *He moves closer to her, as though about to comfort her, then stops*)

HOWARD (*speaking lightly*): Actually, I'm not much good in the way of moral support and I wouldn't have wanted to raise any false hopes . . . Well, goodbye.

LAURA : Goodbye. (HOWARD *picks up his case and goes to french window. He stops, looks back at* LAURA, *who is turned away, then exits by french window and* OFF R. LAURA *slowly walks across the room; she looks very lonely.* MISS TRANSOM *enters R.*)

MISS TRANSOM : I've got it! I've got it! This place used to be a registered Nursing Home! (LAURA *looks mystified*) Well, they've probably still got it on their list of registered Nursing Homes! Don't you understand?

LAURA : No, I don't.

MISS TRANSOM (*cupping her ear*): I can't hear you. I thought I'd left my hearing-aid on the hall-table but it isn't there.

LAURA : I said I don't understand what you mean.

MISS TRANSOM : Well, listen. (*Excitedly—*) What are the regulations about Nursing Homes?

LAURA : They have to be approved by the Health Authorities.

MISS TRANSOM : And would they approve Abbot's Mead—with Miss Prestwood in charge?

LAURA : No. She isn't qualified.

MISS TRANSOM : Exactly! So work it out, my dear! Work it out! (GRAHAM enters U.L. carrying an open briefcase) I wonder if I left my hearing-aid in the reading-room. I'll go and look. (Going L., stops) Don't forget — work it out. (She exits U.L.)

GRAHAM (chuckles): Poor old Thelma! She ought to get herself one of those old-fashioned ear-trumpets. She wouldn't lose that! . . . I don't know, though. (He notices LAURA thinking hard) Something happened, Laura? You look a bit excited about something. (He puts the brief-case on table and rummages inside it)

LAURA : Things are beginning to add up. But why me? Why did she pick on me?

GRAHAM : Who?

LAURA : Miss Prestwood. (She is thinking aloud rather than talking to GRAHAM and she gets more and more worked up as each point emerges) She's behind this stolen jewellery affair. She's a crook and she's using this place as her cover—can you imagine a better one than a private Nursing Home? But Nursing Homes come under the supervision of the Health Authorities and they have to have a qualified person in charge, so after she took over from Miss Lorrimer she tried to get over that by starting to call it a Convalescent Home. That would put it outside the control of the County Health Department, you see? But it isn't as easy as all that and they must have been asking questions about the place. She had to get a qualified nurse in—and that's why she tricked me into coming here.

GRAHAM : No, no — that won't wash.

LAURA : Why not — it fits!

GRAHAM : But — but — I mean she couldn't keep you here indefinitely.

LAURA : She wouldn't need to. Only long enough to put a big deal through—like the Kerrigan diamonds, worth sixty thousand pounds. Then she could clear out. (ELSA enters U.L.)

ELSA : Are you ready, Graham? (She looks from GRAHAM to LAURA) Anything the matter?

GRAHAM : Laura believes that Miss Prestwood tricked her into coming here as a cover-up for a stolen jewellery racket . . . It won't stand up, Laura. Why should she pick on you? She didn't know anything about you.

LAURA : She could have done.

ELSA : How?

LAURA : You remember I wouldn't talk about my life in Dublin? Well, the reason was that I worked for a criminal, for two years. He was a diabetic and needed constant nursing. His name was Jonas Donlevey and he was the receiver of stolen goods that Inspector Kershaw told you about. I hadn't known he was a criminal but I *had* seen the Kerrigan diamonds before. That's why I fainted when they were found in my suitcase the night I came—I recognized them. I had seen Jonas Donlevey putting them away in his safe one day and a few nights later the place was broken into and the diamonds were taken. It was really the shock of that that killed Donlevey but when the Dublin police came in to investigate his affairs they wouldn't believe me. They thought I knew something about the disappearance of the diamonds and they gave me a terrible time. I was called as a witness at the post mortem and my picture was in all the papers. Miss Prestwood could have seen it and read all about me.

GRAHAM : Yes, I suppose she could, but—well, I meantersay it doesn't explain why she picked on you to bring here.

LAURA : I was in trouble. I badly wanted to get out of Ireland and I badly wanted a job. I was easy meat. (GRAHAM *shakes his head doubtfully*) I tell you I'm right! Miss Prestwood's the key to the whole thing and you've got to help me.

ELSA : Help you?

LAURA : Go to the police. Tell them the whole story. Make them check on her.

ELSA : You can tell Inspector Kershaw yourself. (*She seems anxious to be away*)

LAURA : He wouldn't believe me after all that's happened. Go to the County Headquarters—they'll do something.

GRAHAM : I doubt that. After all, you can't give them any proof, can you?

ELSA (*looking at her watch*): Come on, Graham. We haven't much time.

GRAHAM : Okay. Where's my brief-case? (*Goes to table and starts arranging the contents of his brief-case*)

LAURA : Where are you going?

ELSA : We've got to get to London Airport by eleven-thirty.

LAURA : Don't leave me here, Elsa.

ELSA : You'll be all right.

LAURA : Elsa — please!

GRAHAM : Okay, Elsa — let's go.

ANNETTE (OFF L.): You're not going anywhere, Graham. (ELSA and GRAHAM *stop dead. LAURA is unable to believe what she has heard. Then she slowly turns her head and looks towards* ENTR. U.L. ANNETTE *enters, quite slowly*)

LAURA : You! (ANNETTE *never even glances at her*)

ELSA (*in disgust, angrily*): Well, that's that!

LAURA : I never hit you with the car! It was another trick to keep me here! (*Nobody heeds her. She looks round quickly*) Elsa! You're in it! (*She sees* GRAHAM *still busy inside his brief-case, goes to him thrusts her hand into the case and brings out the Kerrigan jewellery*) You're all in it! (*Without grabbing,* GRAHAM *takes hold of her wrist, takes the jewellery and puts it back in the brief-case, then going on to fasten it*)

ANNETTE : Don't try and run out on me, Graham. Not any more.

ELSA (*furiously*): You fool! You little fool! Why didn't you stay out of sight, like you were told?

ANNETTE (*still never taking her eyes off* GRAHAM): You're not going to leave me for that fancy talker, Graham, I won't let you.

ELSA (*savagely, to* GRAHAM): I warned you we could expect trouble from *her*! Why didn't you throw her out when I told you? (MISS PRESTWOOD *enters* U.L. ELSA *turns on her angrily*) Why didn't you keep her in the attic?

MISS PRESTWOOD: I couldn't help it—she promised—

ELSA: This whole job's been on a razor-edge all the time through her! She was so eaten up with jealousy she couldn't even keep her mind on the job enough to avoid being seen outside that cafe in O'Connell Street!

LAURA (*to* ELSA): It was you, wasn't it? You who saw my picture in the paper—you who got the idea to bring me here! And you're a crook like the others!

ELSA (*angrily*): Shut up! (*She goes to* MISS PRESTWOOD)

LAURA: I don't know where you're going but it won't do you any good. I'm going to tell the police everything.

ELSA: What makes you think you'll be able to get out?

LAURA: You can't keep me here for ever.

ELSA: We can keep you long enough. (*To* MISS PRESTWOOD—) And you keep Annette here until Graham and I get to Switzerland, do you understand? I don't care how you do it—lock her up, give her a shot of something—anything. But I'm not going to have her ruining everything now!

MISS PRESTWOOD: I'll see to it.

ANNETTE: She'll be no good to you, Graham. She cares about nobody but herself. She'll ditch you the minute it suits her (ELSA *ignores her, fastening her coat, getting her bag, etc.*)

MISS PRESTWOOD (*pulling* ANNETTE *back*): Keep quiet. Which of you's got the diamonds?

GRAHAM (*patting his brief-case*): I have—right here.

MISS PRESTWOOD: Right—off you go. (LAURA *goes quickly to* french *window. Something she sees* OFF R. *makes her react sharply*)

ELSA: Come on, Graham. (*She finds* LAURA *barring her way*) Out of the way.

LAURA: You're not going.

ELSA: I said get out of the way, or else—

LAURA: Or what? You'll make me? Don't try it, Elsa. Your way was always to get somebody else to do the real work for you, even at school, wasn't it? Of course, you could always call on him, couldn't you? (*Indicating* GRAHAM) He looks as though you've got him pretty well trained.

GRAHAM (*patiently*): Now look—you know you can't stop us leaving.

LAURA: Not for very long, perhaps—

GRAHAM: Then be sensible and move out of the way.

LAURA: —just long enough to let Inspector Kershaw get here.

(KERSHAW *appears from* OFF R. *and she comes downstage*) You won't be catching that 'plane to Switzerland, after all. (KERSHAW *enters*) Inspector—these are the people you want—all four of them.

KERSHAW : Is that so, Miss Harrington?

LAURA : They used me to bring the Kerrigan jewels here and those two were just off to London Airport to fly to Switzerland with them. (*Indicates* ANNETTE) It was all a put-up job about her being hurt by the car last night, just to keep me here. And Miss Prestwood tricked me into coming here so as to stop an investigation by the County Health Authorities. I can prove everything I say.

KERSHAW : Can you now?

LAURA : Yes . . . Well, aren't you going to call your men and arrest them?

KERSHAW : No, Miss Harrington, I'm not.

LAURA : Why not?

KERSHAW : Because I always go to a great deal of trouble to see that none of my operatives ever get arrested. (*To* GRAHAM) The diamonds? (GRAHAM *hands him the briefcase*) Right. You and Elsa call in at the lodge as you go and Stevens will give you your new passports. You'll be travelling as the representatives of a British textile firm and Elsa as your secretary.

LAURA (*aghast*): You — you mean . . .

KERSHAW : Yes, Miss Harrington. I'm what is commonly known as the gang-boss. This is part of my staff—quite efficient, on the whole, though Annette's caused us a bit of trouble by letting her emotions get the better of her. We shall have to watch that sort of thing. It can lead to trouble.

ANNETTE (*wearily*): As far as I'm concerned you can forget it. I'm getting out of it. Goodbye, Graham. Let's just forget it ever happened. (*She exits* U.L. GRAHAM *makes to go after her, then stops*)

KERSHAW : Pity, but perhaps it's just as well.

LAURA : I should have guessed. It was you who changed that note in my handbag last night.

KERSHAW : I didn't change anything. The note you handed me was the genuine one written by Miss Prestwood. I had to improvise. I read out something about a change of meal-times.

LAURA (*bitterly*): If I'd only checked back on the note!

KERSHAW : It was a risk I had to take. But it's my business to take risks. Now Elsa—you know what to do?

ELSA : We'll stay in Geneva until we hear from you that the heat's off. (KERSHAW *nods*)

MISS PRESTWOOD : What about her? (*Indicating* LAURA) We'll have to keep her away from Miss Transom and Millie.

KERSHAW : Put her in the lodge and tell Stevens to keep her locked in a bedroom for a few days. That will give you time to clear things up here, then join me in Dublin.

MISS PRESTWOOD : Very well.

KERSHAW : A pity to give up Abbot's Mead. It's been a perfect cover for quite a long time. Still, it's served its purpose. (*Indicating* LAURA) Bring her along to the lodge. (GRAHAM *takes* LAURA'S *arm*)

LAURA (*shaking him off*): Take your hands off me!

GRAHAM (*seizing her*): Come on!

LAURA (*fighting*): Let me go!

KERSHAW : Don't be a fool, girl! It's either a few days locked in the lodge or we can arranged for you to be disposed of permanently. Take your choice. (LAURA *stops struggling but* GRAHAM *still keeps hold of her arms*) All right, everybody—let's get moving. (*He goes towards french window.* HOWARD *enters by* DOOR R.)

HOWARD : Good morning, Inspector. (KERSHAW *stops dead, then he turns*)

KERSHAW : I was told you'd gone, Mr Carson.

HOWARD : Mm? Well no, I hadn't, actually. I remembered there were one or two people I hadn't said goodbye to.

KERSHAW : I see.

HOWARD : Why is Peters holding Miss Harrington like that?

KERSHAW : I'm afraid Miss Harrington's been behaving a little strangely.

LAURA : They're a gang of crooks and he's their chief! He isn't from Scotland Yard—he's the man who organized the jewel robbery.

KERSHAW (*to* HOWARD) : You see what I mean ? (LAURA *wrenches herself free and runs to* HOWARD)

LAURA : They're clearing out with the Kerrigan diamonds and they're going to lock me up in the lodge !

MISS PRESTWOOD (*in her 'matron's manner'*) : Oh dear, that concussion was quite serious. She's been really violent. (HOWARD *nods*).

LAURA : It isn't true ! Won't you believe me ? Make him open that case—you'll find the jewellery inside.

KERSHAW : But of course you will. What else would a police officer do with stolen property but keep it in his possession ? (*Again* HOWARD *nods*)

LAURA (*almost frantic*) : He's lying, I tell you ! He's lying ! You must believe me—I swear they're crooks—all of them ! Please ! Take me away !

MISS PRESTWOOD (*overlapping*) : Inspector—she's getting worked up again.

KERSHAW : Yes. You'd better go to the lodge and see about a room for Miss Harrington. Tell my men I've sent you.

MISS PRESTWOOD : Yes, Inspector. (*She exits* U.L.)

KERSHAW : Mr Peters. (GRAHAM *goes towards* LAURA)

LAURA : No—No! (*To* HOWARD—) You heard what he said — they're going to lock me up in the lodge ! Make them let me go.

KERSHAW (*regretfully, to* HOWARD): Can't leave her here in that state.

HOWARD : I can't see how I can help very much, Miss Harrington.

ELSA : Don't make it harder for yourself, Laura, please.

LAURA (to HOWARD, desperately): Oh, what can I do to make you believe me—what can I do ?

HOWARD : If you'll take my advice, Miss Harrington, you'll go quietly along with Elsa and try to rest until the doctor comes. Then you'll be all right. (LAURA, who has been keyed up to full tension relaxes and turns despairingly away. ELSA goes to LAURA, GRAHAM puts his arm round her and they take her out by french window OFF R. HOWARD turns away and lights a cigarette)

KERSHAW : A sad business, Mr Carson. (HOWARD nods) Miss Prestwood was right. That knock on the head must have been quite a nasty one. Let's hope she'll soon recover. Well I must be getting along. (He turns upstage)

HOWARD : I'll call you at Scotland Yard, Inspector. (KERSHAW stops. Neither moves for some moments, then KERSHAW turns front)

KERSHAW : I beg your pardon ?

HOWARD : I shall be working at our Head Office in London. I'll call in at the Yard and let you know where you can reach me when you want me.

KERSHAW : Why should I want you, Mr Carson ?

HOWARD : Well, if you're going to lay a charge against Miss Harrington in connection with that stolen jewellery, you'll need my evidence. A statement and all that.

KERSHAW : Oh, I see what you mean. No. no, Mr Carson, there'll be no charge against Miss Harrington. I'm satisfied she's blameless in the matter.

HOWARD : Oh, good.

KERSHAW : Well, I must hurry if I'm going to catch my train. Goodbye, Mr Carson.

HOWARD : Goodbye, Inspector. (KERSHAW exits by french window. HOWARD stands smoking thoughtfully then lays his cigarette in an ashtray. He goes over to R. and looks up at a small picture or wall-ornament which is on the R. wall just inside the door-way, then he takes it down, revealing MISS TRANSOM'S hearing-aid hanging on the same hook, the cord leading out through the doorway. He takes down the hearing-aid, pulling the cord with it, and places it on the table. He is deliberately stubbing out his cigarette in the ashtray when LAURA appears from OFF R. She comes slowly in by french window and stands upstage looking at HOWARD. He watches her in silence)

LAURA : Why didn't you tell me? (HOWARD is silent) Why did you let them . . . ? (She puts her hand to her head. HOWARD goes quickly to her, supports her and brings her to a chair. He puts her in it then pours some water into a glass. He is putting it to her lips when MISS TRANSOM and MILLIE hurry in U.L.)

MISS TRANSOM (excitedly): There are two police-cars in the drive!

MILLIE : The place is simply swarming with coppers!

HOWARD : I know. It's all right.

Miss Transom : What did you say ? Oh, I'm livid not having my hearing-aid at a time like this!

Howard : You'll find it on the table.

Miss Transom (going to table): You found it?

Howard : I borrowed it, Miss Transom. I'm afraid I had to put the standard ear-piece in it.

Miss Transom (plugging it in her ear): Oh, that doesn't matter—I can manage.

Millie : Are all them coppers to do with them diamonds then? (Howard nods) Coo! (She hurries upstage) Come on, Miss T.—let's have a butcher's! (She hurries out by french window)

Miss Transom : Wait for me! (She hurries out. Laura has recovered and Howard puts the glass aside)

Howard : Better now? (Laura nods)

Laura : How long have you known?

Howard : Well, I didn't actually know the whole story until I heard what they've been saying in the last quarter of an hour or so.

Laura : But how could you hear?

Howard : I hung Miss Transom's deaf-aid behind the picture over there, led the cord out round the door frame and listened out in the passage.

Laura : But why?

Howard : I needed all the details for when I give evidence against Kershaw and Co. in court.

Laura : Are you a police-officer?

Howard : Now do I look like a copper?

Laura : I don't know. When it come to police I'll never judge by looks again. (They are both relaxed now) But somehow I don't think I ever really believed you were just a neurotic.

Howard : Oh, didn't you! Well, I thought I was pretty good—in fact, there were times when I almost convinced myself. (Laura laughs) If you really want to know, I'm an insurance investigator.

Laura : Now why didn't I think of that? As if I ever would.

Howard : For quite a while there's been a series of claims for jewel robberies that seemed to follow a pattern. We got some leads that kept coming back to Abbot's Mead but never anything strong enough to give to the police. Finally, I thought the only way was for me to check in as a patient and see if it would lead me to the top man. It paid quite a dividend, didn't it? (Miss Transom appears at french window)

Miss Transom : They're packing them into the police-cars, the whole boiling of them! Oh, isn't it exciting? Now I know what you were doing out there last night.

Howard : Do you?

Miss Transom : Yes. You went out to telephone the police, didn't you? And I know how you got out of the grounds, too.

Howard : You tell me.

Miss Transom (triumphantly): Through the old air-raid shelter that leads under the wall and out into the spinney.

HOWARD (*laughs*): You're a cunning old witch.

MISS TRANSOM (*chuckles gleefully*): Yes, aren't I? Oh, I've had such fun the last two days! (*She scurries out by french window*)

LAURA : Well, I'm glad somebody has. Was she right about the police?

HOWARD : Yes. They've been watching the place all night, under cover. When Kershaw got here this morning they moved in. Well, that's about it. I'll have to get over to County Police H.Q. and sign a statement.

LAURA (*a little wistfully*): Just another case closed? (*She gets up and moves a few paces* DOWN L. HOWARD *looks round at her*)

HOWARD : No. Not just another case closed.

LAURA : Why not?

HOWARD (*coming to her*): Because of you, I suppose.

LAURA : Why me?

HOWARD : Well, it's a bit difficult to explain. How shall I put it? How about like this? (*Takes her in his arms and kisses her*)

LAURA (*in relief*): Oh, if you'd only done that before I could have coped so much better with all those terrible things that were happening to me.

HOWARD : Tell you what—come with me while I sign that statement for the County Police, then we'll hop into the car and drive until the petrol gives out.

LAURA : How much petrol have you got in?

HOWARD : Ten gallons.

LAURA : We'll be driving all day!

HOWARD : That's the general idea. (*They laugh and* HOWARD *briefly kisses* LAURA *again.* MILLIE *enters* R, *followed by* MISS TRANSOM)

MILLIE : There's a man here from the County Health Department

MISS TRANSOM : He's come to inspect Abbot's Mead and he wants to see the person in charge—

MILLIE : That means you, Miss Harrington. (HOWARD *takes* LAURA'S arm and hurries her L.)

LAURA (*calling back, at* ENTR. U.L.): Tell him I've resigned! (*She and* HOWARD *exit quickly* U.L., *leaving* MILLIE *staring in bewildered helplessness, while* MISS TRANSOM *chuckles in high glee*)

CURTAIN

THE END

PROPERTY LIST
ACT ONE

On Stage :

> On a small table, telephone.
>
> In vases, autumn flowers.
>
> On coffee-table, or other small table, box of cigarettes.

Personal :

> HOWARD : A small, partly-woven basket. Empty cigarette-packet, matches.
>
> GRAHAM : Shooting-stick. Pipe, pouch, matches.
>
> MISS TRANSOM : An open-topped workbag. In it, a transistor hearing-aid with cord to earpiece.
>
> LAURA : Handbag. In it the key to her week-end case. Week end case. In it, some garments and the Kerrigan jewellery.
>
> KERSHAW : Wallet. Pipe, pouch, matches. Note-book. Ball-point pen.

Off Stage L.:

> FOR MILLIE : Her handbag and coat. Glass with a little water in. Basin. In it a face-cloth.
>
> FOR GRAHAM : Country-style walking stick.
>
> FOR ELSA : Her coat.

ACT TWO. Scene I.

Personal :

> FOR MILLIE : Dustette hand-vacuum, long-handled polishing-mop or other cleaning appliance.
>
> MISS TRANSOM : Her hearing-aid.
>
> HOWARD : Cigarettes and lighter.
>
> KERSHAW : Notebook, ball-point.
>
> LAURA : Her hand-bag. In it, a number of quarto-sized sheets of letter-paper, fastened together at the top left-hand corner.

ACT TWO. Scene II.

Personal :

> GRAHAM : Pipe, pouch, matches.
>
> MILLIE : Duster.
>
> HOWARD : Cigarettes, Lighter. Bunch of keys.
>
> LAURA : Her handbag. In it a pocket-diary and, in that a folded slip of paper.

ACT THREE. Scene I.

Personal :

> MISS TRANSOM : Her hearing-aid.
>
> GRAHAM : Pipe, pouch, matches.

Off Stage R.:

> FOR MISS TRANSOM : Open-topped workbag. In it, a comb, a bunch of keys, the Kerrigan jewellery.

Off Stage L.:

> FOR LAURA : Her coat and handbag.

ACT THREE. Scene II.

Set :

Miss Transom's hearing-aid behind the picture near Door R.,
the cord being led out, at ear-level, round the door-frame
and loosely hooked out of sight beyond Door R.

Carafe of water and some glasses on a tray on a side-table.

Personal :

For Graham : Brief-case. In it, the Kerrigan jewellery.

For Howard : Cigarettes and lighter.

Off Stage L.:

For Howard : Filled suitcase or holdall.

LIGHTING

ACT ONE : the concealed lighting beyond the window shows the
dim light of early evening. Inside the room all the onstage
visible lights are on.

ACT TWO, Scene I and Scene II : None of the room-lights are
on and the room is presumed to be illuminated by daylight.
Beyond the window, morning sunlight.

ACT THREE, Scene I.: All the onstage visible lights are lit. Beyond the window the concealed lighting shows the dark blue
of night. Scene II : As for ACT TWO.

ENTRANCES AND EXITS

Throughout the play all characters re-enter from the same side
of the stage (L. or R.) as that by which they made their exits;
there is thus no need to provide for space behind the back wall
for them to change over out of sight of the audience.

R. means Right when facing the audience.

L. means Left when facing the audience.

C. means Centre.

Upstage means that part of the stage furthest away from the
audience.

Downstage means that part of the stage nearest the audience.

PRODUCTION NOTES

As the play has to develop into one of tension later on, it is important not to strike a false note in the earlier stages. There should be no obvious 'playing for laughs' while the foundations of ACT ONE are being laid, or the audience will be sidetracked into being unprepared for the dramatic developments of the mystery surrounding LAURA. This does not mean that there should be no comedy but that it should be comedy arising out of the character not comic 'business' added to it. Thus MILLIE will get legitimate comedy by being outspoken, cheerful, self-possessed without overdoing the 'cheekiness'; MISS TRANSOM should use her slyness and witch-like chuckle to establish the character and to get laughs but must tone these down at moments of suspense or when some necessary information has to be got over to the audience.

Care is needed in the case of HOWARD. It would be easy to read facetiousness into his lines but this is the very quality to be avoided in this play. He has to be slightly irritable without appearing ill-mannered; short-tempered but not bad-tempered. He must keep the audience on his side and yet, at the points demanded by the text, behave in a manner that will cause them to suspect him. With GRAHAM he is sarcastic, not flippant. He is self-possessed and cool but when an unexpected situation arises he should be seen to be seriously concerned about it. GRAHAM should play in an easy, unforced style, bringing out the 'old-boy' style of conversation without making a meal of it. He should bring out his keennes for ELSA rather more than his lines seem to do. His attitude to ANNETTE is not impatience (except perhaps, in his last scene with her) but the kind of awkwardness that an easy-going man would show with a girl he was trying to 'let down lightly'. In ACT ONE he should 'point' the reference to his leg only by bending his knee once or twice and on no account should he limp or even lean heavily on his stick.

ELSA should be rather more vivacious than her lines might indicate; very charming and good-humoured and anxious to be a good friend to LAURA. In the last ACT 'show-down' she presents a greater contrast than any of the others—intensely angry with ANNETTE and MISS PRESTWOOD, contemptuous of LAURA and dominating GRAHAM. In the case of MISS PRESTWOOD it is vital that the words "prim" and "fussy" applied to her in the text are not to be taken in the comedy sense, for she must on no account be played as a comedy character. In this context "prim" means "rather precise in manner" and "fussy" means "conscientious". In other words she must be a thoroughly believable, pleasant, kindly woman, capable and friendly to everyone.

The Producer should ensure that LAURA makes a good entrance (none of HOWARD's 'business' being allowed to detract from it) and try to get across to the audience that, with her arrival, things are going to start happening. She should take whatever opportunities there are to vary her moods—a smile or laugh where the situation permits it—and not to go into extremes of tension and fear too early on or she will have nothing left in hand with which to hold the audience as the suspense of the play mounts later on. She must engage the sympathy of the audience throughout.

ANNETTE has little or no chance to show any light-heartedness but even so she ought not to play all her scenes with GRAHAM in the same key. At first she has some hope, then rather less, finally she accepts the situation in a dull, resigned kind of despair. She should be nicely dressed and look attractive on each appearance. KERSHAW will be a much more interesting character if, instead of the usual efficient and colourless run-of-the-mill detective, he is genial and amiable (almost fatherly, if the actor is of that age), except where the situation requires otherwise. But he should not be over-hearty with it.

Changes of costume between ACTS and SCENES will convey to the audience the passing of time, even if it is only the change of a man's sports jacket to a cardigan.

MISS TRANSOM's hearing-aid is about three inches by four, either the light beige colour of the N.H.S. type or else a flat tin, painted gold to represent a luxury model. It should have a clip to fasten it to MISS TRANSOM's belt or dress. At the other end of the cord the earpiece could be contrived with a small cork with the top covered with a piece of pink plastic. For the last ACT, Scene 2, this (or a duplicate) should be concealed behind a picture (or wall ornament, or even a light-fixture) which blends in with others on the walls. On no account must it be so ill-sited that it screams aloud to the audience that there is something fishy about it. (A wall-fitment containing a small potted plant might be practicable), or some trailing ivy could conceal the cord.) The cord should be hooked loosely at ear-level out of sight behind the door-frame.

The Kerrigan jewellery should be as glittering and flashy as possible and there should be a big enough quantity of it to make it look effective to the audience. It might be prudent to have the pieces tied to each other with thread so as to ensure HOWARD bringing them all out together in a handful without some of it falling back.

The french window and the window curtains remain open throughout the play.

In ACT TWO, Scene I, where KERSHAW explains about his investigation, this should not be allowed to get static or it will drag, and bore the audience. KERSHAW should vary the pace—slowing down to get an important item across, etc., and some of his listeners could be given just a little suitable 'business' or reaction so that they do not look like a class listening to a lecture.

At the passages indicated, some work should be put in on the incidents where it is desired to cause the audience to suspect HOWARD. Similarly, great care should be taken that ELSA, GRAHAM, MISS PRESTWOOD and KERSHAW do nothing in the least suspicious until their true characters are exposed in ACT THREE, Scene 2 (earlier for MISS PRESTWOOD, of course).

At the end of ACT TWO, Scene 2, MISS TRANSOM's appearance should be unmasked and, on this occasion, she may be "straight" and not her usual witch-like self.

In the ACT THREE, Scene 2 "showdown," ELSA, GRAHAM, MISS PRESTWOOD and KERSHAW are hard, ruthless and *practical* professional criminals engaged in the last stage of their operation. They do not dawdle about or indulge in crime-fiction banter or mockery of their victim.

LAURA's last entrance should be designed for visual effect—slow walk, expressionless face, etc.—and HOWARD should focus the audience's attention on it by keeping fairly still and looking upstage, watching LAURA all the time. She is neither frightened nor elated, but rather still numbed by what has happened. Fairly soon, though not too abruptly, she is able to relax and she and HOWARD end the play on a happy note though not too light-heartedly so.

Printed by The Galloway Gazette Press, Newton Stewart.